If the Cap Fits

My Rocky Road to Emmerdale

STEVE HALLIWELL

The
History
Press

For Valerie

To the women I have lived with and loved: Jenny, my mother; Susan, my first wife; Valerie, my second wife; Charlotte, my daughter; Lisa, my ex-girlfriend; Valerie – a second time.

Front cover illustration © Amy Brammall

First published 2014

This edition published 2017 by

The History Press
The Mill, Brimscombe Port
Stroud, Gloucestershire, GL5 2QG
www.thehistorypress.co.uk

© Steve Halliwell, 2014, 2017

The right of Steve Halliwell to be identified as the Author
of this work has been asserted in accordance with the
Copyright, Designs and Patents Act 1988.

British Library Cataloguing in Publication Data.
A catalogue record for this book is available from the British
Library.

ISBN 978 0 7509 6991 8

Typesetting and origination by The History Press
Printed and bound by CPI Group (UK) Ltd

Contents

Foreword

To all those whom I may have hurt or harmed in my life, I humbly ask for forgiveness. To all those who have hurt or harmed me, I forgive unreservedly. I do not in any way want to glamorise excessive drinking in this book. Where heavy drinking features, it is simply because it is integral to my story, so has to be told if I am to be honest. Heavy drinking has actually caused more harm than good in my life. Part of the sequence of events might be mixed up due to memory failure.

Many thanks to Sandra Kocinski. The sixties black-and-white photographs are by George Broadbent.

Special thanks to Sean Frain, the Bury-born writer, for his help, advice and guidance in producing this book. His works include: *The Bury Book of Days, Bury Murders, Cumbrian True Crimes: Murder & Mystery in the Lakes, The Lake District: A Visitor's Miscellany* and many more.

Who Am I?

Make it thy business to know thyself, which is the most difficult lesson in the world.

Miguel de Cevantes

I was 18 years old. It was 1964 and I found myself staring hard at my reflection in the Trafalgar Square Wash and Brush-Up, feeling free at last. I had absolutely no idea where I was going, or what I would do with my life, nor had I any idea of how I was going to survive. But this situation felt strangely natural: I was doing the right thing. I certainly felt better about myself than when I was standing at the end of a factory production line, living the life of an automaton.

Often alone, I would walk the streets looking for money or food, but I found London to be fiercely hostile to the penniless. Hours passed as I walked my usually unfruitful walk, but still I held on to the feeling that walking those streets for eight hours was far better than standing at the end of a mind-numbing production line for eight hours. It had almost driven me mad. Perhaps it had driven me completely mad and that is why I found myself alone, hungry and skint – virtually living the life of a tramp.

During the dark nights, I sometimes climbed over the fences of private gardens in exclusive squares surrounded by Georgian houses and I would sleep in the bushes, knowing that I could only be disturbed by someone taking their dog for an early-morning walk, before work. I never was disturbed, despite this being a regular part of my routine. During those walks I would sometimes glance through restaurant windows with hunger knots in my stomach, wondering if I would ever be able to eat in such fine places. It wasn't out of envy that I would look into those comfortable, affluent scenes, for never would I want to be on the other side peering out at someone like myself, with such a disdainful expression on my face. I was hungry, that's all. Fish and chips or a cheese sandwich would have served me just as well as fine dining. I wanted to eat, and, more importantly, to know what I was going to do with the rest of my life. I wanted to know what I, Steve Halliwell, would become.

My mother told me that I was conceived at Billy Butlin's holiday camp at Filey, Yorkshire, but I was born on 19 March 1946 at 40 Lord Street, a red-brick terraced house built for mill workers at Heap Bridge, on the edge of the town of Bury in Lancashire. The village consisted of a few streets and factories, two churches, two public houses (both now closed), a working men's club, one school, four shops, a stretch of river and a railway line, which were surrounded by fields and hill pastures at the foot of the bleak Pennines.

Some of my earliest memories are of going to the local shop for mother, carrying a ration book, which continued to be issued for several years after the Second World War had ended. I would often deliberately set off in the wrong direction just to hear Mum shouting, 'Ferguson's, not Yates's.' I didn't see a great deal of Fred Halliwell, my father, as he spent twelve long hours a day working in a nearby mill – the Transparent Paper Mill – which gave employment to many folk in the area. This man, who sat in the chair reading his newspaper, smoking and mutely demanding silence from my brother and I, was a mysterious figure to me.

My brother, Clive, is two years my senior and we both have many memories of those times, yet when we meet up we hardly ever talk about our childhood. Christmas, bonfire night, whit walks, and the occasional and welcome holiday in a wooden chalet at Gronant in North Wales were undoubtedly the highlights of my childhood, but I suppose the long summer holidays wandering the fields and countryside surrounding our village were the happiest and most memorable times. Looking back on those whit walks I can remember the gathering afterwards at Hamilton's farm field where we had egg and spoon races, three-legged races and many other peculiarly eccentric games.

We rented our house, which was a small two-up, two-down with no bathroom and an outside toilet, known as a privy. The coal fire was the focal point of our evenings and the family would sit around it, sometimes in silence, sometimes listening to the radio – *Al Read*, *The Billy Cotton Band Show*, *Archie Andrews* and *Forces Favourites*. TV then was still only a dream. My mind would drift freely during the silent intervals as I conjured up boyhood fantasies from the caves and crevices of red and yellow coals glowing in the hearth, the lights from the flames flickering and dancing across the walls around our tiny living room.

I suppose, materially, ours was an average working-class household common to those times. We had basic food, basic clothing, basic affection, but, for some reason, very little fun together. My mother suffered from polio as a child, which had left her lame in one leg. She was the eldest daughter of Harold

Moss, an ex-coal miner who had become very well known in the world of northern brass bands. When still a young man he was known as King of the Trombone and by the time I was born he was a bandmaster for Leyland Motors. Several times he adjudicated at the annual National Brass Band Contest at the Royal Albert Hall. He composed and arranged many pieces and was also a teacher of music.

My mother, Mary Jane, was known to all as Jenny and she often played our piano. Debussy's wonderful 'Clair de Lune' was my favourite, and still, whenever I hear it, I'm taken back in an instant to when I first heard it at my mother's side. As young boys, my brother and I, alongside the other kids we knocked about with, would spend hours throwing stones into the stinking mounds of chemical foam which meandered along the river. When I was a child I thought all fish came from the sea; I didn't realise our river should have been full of life. It had died due to all the factory waste that had been tipped in there over the years. Despite all of these things, we kids never questioned the quality of life we had in those days. Children, it seems to me, accept their lot much more easily than do adults. Michael Hopkins was a prime example of this.

He lived across the street with his father and he had difficulty speaking. We sometimes played in his house; games like hide and seek. His father wasn't too house-proud, however, as the bucket used to save nightly trips to the outside toilet wasn't emptied on a regular basis. In fact, it was often so full that it was close to overflowing. His father was more in the pub than at home with his son and I felt sorry for the lad.

The Brooks family also lived across the street and amongst them were Billy, Edwin, Lena and Roy. They often had no heating and Lena and Roy, both around the same age as me, would sit around the open gas oven in an attempt to keep warm. I didn't join in, but some of the other kids laughed at Roy's birthday party, simply because his mum could only afford to put on chips, with jelly for dessert. 'Jelly and chips' was the taunt of several children for days after that party.

We had no bathroom and on hot summer days my mother would drag the old tin bath into our dirt yard at the back of our house, and then plonk me and my brother into its silvery depths. As we grew up, any other baths we had were at the local swimming pool in Bury. People then were not as obsessed with bodily hygiene as they are nowadays. Different friends had different smells – mostly unpleasant ones! Kids with nits; nurses known as 'Nitty-Nora the Bug Explorer'; bitten fingernails; speech impediments; fathers with missing fingers, or missing arms even, all lost in industrial accidents; stunted women with bow legs due to rickets; fleas in our beds – these are just some of the early memories which have remained with me across the decades.

Sundays at that time were spent going to the early-morning service with Mum, who was very much involved with the local church, as she was quite a religious person. Dad, on the other hand, was an atheist. This situation set up very early confusion in my mind about what to believe and what not to believe. I had quite strong spiritual feelings as a young lad and listened with a lot of interest to the stories which were told in church, but the biblical phrase 'do unto others as you would have them do unto you' left a vivid impression and remains with me to this day. It is the one and only teaching I find hard to fault, though, of course, it is difficult to live up to. Even though that ideal was always in my mind, I still managed to get involved in quite a number of fights when I was a young lad. I never mentioned such fights at home, however, for fear of Mother's disapproval. Dad, on the other hand, enjoyed boxing as a spectator.

This confusion regarding religious beliefs wasn't helped when I noticed the hypocrisy of the church. They would preach that it was proper to give one of your two coats to your brother in need, yet poverty was rife all around and I didn't see the church giving up much to help the poor. I wondered why our vicar didn't give up his large four-bedroom house to the Stone family, who had, if my memory serves me correctly, eight children. They somehow had to manage in a two-bedroom house. Surely giving up the large house to that family would have been the Christian thing to do! I believe that leading by example is the best way of teaching. That vicar's example, it seemed to me, had taught nothing of any positive value.

The Drakes* were a really tough family who lived up our street. There were four brothers among them – Terry, Raymond, Richard and Johnny, who all fought like caged tigers, so they were generally the leaders of the kids in our village. And thus their often dodgy activities became the pursuits of us lesser mortals. Setting fire to meadows and fields was a major summer amusement and my brother, Clive, proved more inventive than the rest of our gang. He devised a way of setting fire to the grass so that we could watch from the safety of the distant railway bridge, which was known as Twenty-three Steps. Clive would light a cigarette pinched from our dad's packet when he wasn't looking, lay it in the grass, pile a few matches part-way along and then pile some dry grass on top of that. As the cigarette burned down towards the matches – bingo! – field or meadow was soon ablaze. We called this field-burning activity 'swealing' – I recently looked in the dictionary and it turns out that it is a genuine word, which surprised me.

The railway line running through our village was a little branch line which ran into Duxbury's Paper Mill, in order that trains could bring in pulp and then take out the finished paper. Ernie Hardman was a kid of my age who lived at the other end of our terrace. One day he and I hung onto the buffers of a

---

* Note this name has been changed here and throughout to protect identities.

slowly moving train, laughing hysterically at our own stupidity. We rode the buffers until we could hold on no longer and then dropped onto the railway tracks, watching the little steam engine clang and puff away into the distance. We would then hurry to tell our friends of our latest achievement. Walking across a pipe which crossed the river was another dare that all the boys in our village had to do – if they wanted to fit in, that is. If not, they would then forever be branded a 'soft-arse'.

One way or another I always seemed to find myself in trouble and, as a result, I was given the cane at school almost as many times as a mate of mine named Barry Nicholson, who also had a reputation as a troublesome lad. When I had almost attained the kudos of being the most caned boy in school, 'Baz' would always go and beat me to it. There was an old piano in his home too and he could play it by ear, as he was a naturally talented musician. He enjoyed singing and would do so very loudly as he walked to and from the local shop. In later years he became a club singer whose stage name is Barry Gee.

Another early showbiz influence was Keith Smith. He would perform wherever and whenever he got the chance. He would sing a song, play the mouth organ and one of his finest party pieces was doing Hilda Baker impressions. He was only about 10 years of age at the time, but he already had business cards printed which announced: Keith Smith – the Wonderboy of Heywood. Every Saturday morning I would get my spending money and walk from Heap Bridge to Bury town centre in order to watch the morning Odeon screening, which was known as the kids club. One Saturday Keith and I were in the cinema and, because he didn't want to miss any of the film by having to go off to the toilet, he urinated under the seats instead, which I found hysterical at the time. No wonder those old cinemas stank so awful.

One Saturday a pea-souper smog, a mixture of low cloud and smoke from the hundreds of mills and factories in the area, descended on our village. These terrible smogs were very bad for the health and caused severe breathing problems in some cases; later legislation was passed which enforced smokeless zones. I was 10 years old at the time of the pea-souper and I had never witnessed anything like it before. I could hardly see more than a few inches in front of me. I decided I would go outside and 'disappear' into the gloom, becoming the 'invisible man' or, I should say, 'invisible boy'. I walked very slowly and carefully to the churchyard, which was near our house, and I noticed what looked like bits of soot mixed in with the fog. It was incredibly dense and the eerie silence was just a bit scary.

I then decided I would shout out anything that came into my head. I bellowed from the thick gloom as there was no fear of being identified. I shouted whatever I wanted, including 'FOGBALLS!' after I had wondered if the fog could be made into balls, as one could do with snow. Of course, I knew this wasn't possible, but my imagination ran away with me in that surreal setting. I also shouted, 'I'M NOT 'ERE!', though I don't know why.

After this bout of acting the goat, as Mum would call it, I began to wonder if any of my family were lost in this smog, so I set off for home, but had to tread very carefully in order to avoid bumping into the trees. I thought I would enjoy just one last shout as I neared the house, so 'TIT!!' echoed around the village before silence prevailed once more. When I went inside, my brother was home, but he never mentioned hearing a lunatic shouting in the smog. Mum returned from the nearby shop; then Dad got home from work and Sandy, our cat, suddenly appeared at the door, so everyone was safe.

I also have a vivid memory of jumping out of bed late one night and going over to the window in order to see the red glow of a steam train chuffing along the distant tracks as it blew its whistle. I must have been only about 4 or 5 years of age at the time, yet I imagined those distant trains were heading off to far-flung places such as America, France, Australia and other exciting foreign lands. I can remember thinking, One day, when I am older, I will get on one of those trains and set off on an adventure. These memories still evoke that far-off childhood dream – of things yet to be discovered, of a future yet to be lived. Alas, it wasn't long before I found out those trains were just going up the line to Rochdale, about 6 miles from our home.

Both my grandfathers had been coal miners and I can think of no better way of describing their work than as slavery. I visited the mining museum at Wakefield years later, in 2012, and was utterly disbelieving of what my grandfathers were expected to do each working day. For most miners there was no other way of keeping a roof over their heads and food in their bellies. My father and uncle hadn't gone down the mines, but they still had to graft long hours in order to make a living. This incredibly hard way of life left a lasting impression on me and I felt I had to find another way of living. I was determined that I was not going to be yet another 'slave'. But how could I free myself? It seemed an overwhelming task.

Glynn Harman was another childhood hero of mine. He was about a year older than me and proved to be a good foot-baller and a good fighter. He also had a knack of finding bird nests, as he was good at climbing trees, as well as digging out underground dens and making bows and arrows. He had three older brothers who had taught him all these tricks. Some of my earliest memories are of him taking me to farms where we would steal apples and turnips. Glynn later became a profes-sional footballer.

That small settlement known as Heap Bridge produced some real characters, none of whom could be described as boring. Glynn was small, strong and wiry. He usually spoke fluently, but occasionally stammered in his speech. One day we were walking through some fields far from home when he suddenly stopped and said, 'Sssssnipes nest in fields like this.' He was right too, as one flapped away rapidly after we disturbed it. Glynn found its nest and we arrived home later with an egg each. We blew them in his backyard after putting a pin-hole through both ends. Robbing nests was common among young lads in those days, but is now thankfully rare (as well as highly illegal, not to mention cruel). Glynn also made spears, catapults and pea guns, which were useful for firing at the backs of heads!

Another clear memory I have is of walking in the fields one hot summer's day with Glynn, my brother, Clive, and a few other lads, when we were joined by a stray dog we named Dirt Boy. He remained with us all that hot, shimmering day with the sun beating down on a countryside in full summer glory. But as we arrived back at the village, the dog, for some unknown reason, ran straight under a passing truck and was killed instantly. All of us tried to be macho by holding back the tears, as being tough and seemingly unemotional was the norm in those days, just after the Second World War. This is possibly why Mum teaching me to be quiet and Christian in nature was always at odds with the peer pressure of what was expected of me as a working-class lad in a working-class village.

One Christmas my brother and I were given boxing gloves and we would box each other in the house or in the backyard. Other lads would come round and we would have mini-tournaments. Clive and I were in the house having a few rounds one day when his sock started to hang loose and I must have stood on it at the same time as I threw a cracking straight left – Clive was literally knocked out of his sock. Dad, who was watching from round his newspaper, let out a rare laugh. I felt sorry for my brother as he was clearly angry, him being two years older than me. However, he later made me pay for that punch, during a backyard three-rounder, which was the beginning of my long drawn-out nose-flattening process.

It wasn't until years later, in fact, that I found out that the district of Heap Bridge was considered a no-go area by young lads from other parts of Bury. We had a reputation of being 'hard-nuts', but this particular 'hard-nut' child spent some lonely nights silently crying, so as not to disturb his brother, who was sleeping in the next bed. I was sad, confused and frustrated by my seemingly loveless father, my religious mother and my introvert brother. I didn't know how on earth I could help them to be happy, or myself for that matter. It never dawned on me then that almost everyone is unhappy a lot of the time.

There were always some things to look forward to though, such as the whit walks, which helped take our minds off the harder side of life. St George's Church always employed a Scottish Pipe Band at such times and one of the highlights was seeing the bonny girls in their kilts, velvet jackets and plaid socks. They seemed such exotic creatures and I always imagined they had come all the way down from Scotland just to be with us. So I was a bit disappointed to find out that they came from Oldham, just a few miles up the road. I went to Heap Bridge Primary School and behind it were some old air raid shelters, underground concrete bunkers that had been built during the Second World War. They were very damp, smelly and cold. I don't know who first came up with the idea, but we took to piling dry grass in the shelters and setting it alight. The object of this game was to see who could stay in the shelter the longest, despite suffering from the effects of smoke inhalation. Most would come running out with deep barking coughs and streaming eyes, only to be jeered at for giving in too easily. I am certain that was a contest I never won.

Clive and I did, however, win quite a number of bogey races, racing in a very fast cart built by our dad, using wheels from our old pram. I would push while Clive steered and these races usually took place on the Oller, which may have been the Lancashire rendering of 'hollow'. It was just a bit of spare land. Bonfires were lit on the Oller in November, as well as at Waterfold Lane and on Lord Street, where I lived. These had to be carefully guarded, as lads from other areas, or even our own, would attempt to raid and steal the wood.

A huge fight kicked off one Saturday afternoon when a gang of lads from Prettywood, a district less than a quarter of a mile from Heap Bridge, raided our Lord Street bonfire. My brother received a cut under his eye during a stick fight and this raised conflicting emotions in me. Should I turn the other cheek, as I had been recently taught in church, or should I get stuck in? The matter was quickly settled for me by a blinding migraine attack as the Prettywood gang got away with quite a lot of our wood. One year the Lord Street and Oller gangs pooled their resources in the hope of enjoying one enormous bonfire. We were all sat around a little camp fire one evening as we guarded the precious wood. Richard Drake arrived and suggested we all had a walk over to Seven Arches. We didn't usually disagree with the Drakes, so we set off down Waterfold Lane. Someone then shouted, 'It's a race,' so off we sprinted like whippets, but by the time we reached the first of the seven arches, we realised Richard had disappeared. Fearing the worst, we ran back towards the village and ahead we could see billowing smoke and the glow of fierce flames lighting up the night sky. Richard had hidden paraffin and had then sneaked back and lit up the Oller. Despite a fire engine being called to the scene, we lost all of the wood we had been collecting for several weeks – and this with only two days to go till 5 November. This wasn't the first or last time someone would set light to our bonfire before the official date had arrived.

Another game we played around this time was very dangerous, to say the least. This was dropping bangers down cellar grids and the biggest dare was to drop one down into Walsh's cellar, the local greengrocers, as Jim Walsh would definitely chase us. If he caught any of us we would receive a good hiding for our troubles. One night I plucked up some courage after much goading and dropped a banger down that cellar – the loud echoing blast set us off running. The sense of fear was overwhelming. 'Come 'ere you buggers.' Big Jim, as he was known, was out, running like a madman and gaining on us. I sprinted into the church grounds to try to make my getaway through the trees. However, my heart was pounding like a steam-hammer. I thought I was going to have a heart attack, so I dropped into the long grass and rolled down the hill, hoping that he couldn't see me in the dark. It was then that I heard it: a blood-curdling scream, which meant that one of the lads had been caught and was receiving a good thrashing from Mr Walsh.

Sometimes, on a Saturday afternoon, a gang of us lads would walk to Ashworth Valley, where we enjoyed steep woodland walks. At times we would start out at Heywood and walk back up the banks of the River Roch to Bury, all the while playing cowboys and Indians, or Robin Hood, or whatever we had seen that morning at the Odeon cinema. Sometimes just my brother and I would go and we got to know every inch of Ashworth Valley, including all the different ways of crossing the river, which in places was very shallow. We had an old tent and occasionally my brother and I would camp overnight. Clive had an air rifle and I had an air pistol, so we would set up camp, light the fire and then play cowboys and Indians.

We would also place tin mugs and plates around the fire and Clive would shoot at these from nearby trees while I took cover behind some rocks. I would fire through the trees, pretending to shoot at Clive, and could hear the pellets rattling through the leaves. All of these shoot-outs were in imitation of the cowboy films we had seen at the cinema. I suppose it was quite dangerous, but we never thought about such things at the time. Clive was a very good shot and on one occasion he aimed at and hit an empty pop bottle that was very close to my head. Some of the shattered glass actually hit me in the face, but thankfully I sustained no serious wounds.

When we finally settled down and went to sleep we would take the hot stones from around the camp fire and put our feet on them for warmth. I would drift off, dreaming that I was tired from the day's cattle drive across the prairie. In the morning we would open a tin of beans and place the tin directly on the fire, which would warm them up very nicely. We would sometimes end our walk through the valley at a district known as Fairfield, or sometimes we would walk on to another district, Walmersley, from where we would then walk home to Heap Bridge. When I first went on this walk there was a small café in the woods known as Nab's Wife (a corruption of the area originally known as Nab's Wharfe), where you could get a refreshing cup of tea and a Mars bar. You could also get a bacon butty, but we never had enough money for such 'luxuries'. On one occasion I persuaded Mum to give Clive and me enough money for a bacon butty each, but when we got to the café it was all boarded up and, sadly, never reopened.

I really enjoyed watching cowboy films on these Saturday visits to the cinema, but there were so many random deaths in these films that I spent some of my time worrying about the families of those guys who were always getting shot in saloons or livery stables, even though these characters were baddies, often described as 'dry-gulching sidewinders' or 'bushwacking coyotes'. I also worried about the Indian braves who were usually just left lying around for the vultures. Such little respect for human life really confused me – and it still does today. Those were only movies, but there seems to be just as little respect in real life.

Being a lad from a small village, I believe I had quite a narrow view of life, but things were about to change. I had failed my Eleven Plus exam, which ruled out grammar school, though my brother had managed to get into Rochdale Technical School. My uncle Albert, brother to my dad, also worked at Transparent Paper Mill, but he had progressed to Personnel Manager, so he had been able to send my cousin Keith to a small fee-paying school in Prestwich, south of Bury and not far from Manchester. So Mum, not wanting to be outdone by Uncle Albert, sent me for an entrance exam. I tried desperately to fail it, as I wanted to go to Regent Street School in Heywood, where all of the other lads from the village were going. However, to my horror, they said I had just managed to scrape through. Scrape through? I'd hardly answered any questions and those I did I deliberately answered wrongly. They had obviously passed me simply to get the school fees. This signalled the death-knell of my bond with the other lads. In no time at all 'Snob', 'College Boy' and 'Soft Arse' had all been chalked on our end terrace wall. It was bad enough my brother going to Rochdale Technical School, but me setting off every day in a *maroon blazer* was, to them at least, unforgiveable.

My first day at the school, Cliff Grange, was also my first time in long trousers. I am sure they were made of horse hair, or some similar material, as they rubbed my legs raw. My new shoes were made of plastic. Mum thought they looked very smart. The school building was an enormous detached house that had been converted into several classrooms and the founder and head teacher lived upstairs in a flat.

As I walked through the door on that first morning I noticed a lot of special needs children queuing up. This made me begin wondering if I had been tricked into going to this school, perhaps because Mum and Dad thought I was deranged. Perhaps they had always known that it was me shouting 'tit' in the fog and they had decided I wasn't a 'full shilling'. I certainly felt that I didn't belong. The school seemed very Dickensian and gloomy, especially during times when we lined up in the cellar, or ate our meals down there. During school dinners I was advised to get my 'dinner pocket' ready, which meant having a plastic bag in my blazer pocket ready to put food in. This baffled me to begin with, but I soon realised why this was common practice. We were all expected to clear our plates and the food, unfortunately, was disgusting. One meal served to us was nicknamed 'barley and bizz'. I don't know exactly what it was, but I would in no way be surprised to hear that it was rat and barley. This disgusting concoction was usually served alongside cold boiled potatoes and was enough to put you off food for life. Another 'horror' dish was 'the rissole', which was about as appetising as a dog turd. Rissoles usually ended up in the dinner pocket bag and were later thrown over the fence into the grounds of the neighbouring residence. This gave rise to the legend of the 'rissole tree', as dozens of rissoles in bags hung from its many branches.

During one lesson we were asked to write descriptions of our homes and one kid told me that he couldn't remember the colour of his bathroom suite. I could not join him in such trivialities, however, as we didn't have a bathroom of any colour. So I lied and said ours was green and red.

I felt a little less out of place a year or so later, when Barry and Peter Tracey began attending the school. They were the sons of John Tracey, who was the landlord of the Boar's Head public house in Heap Bridge. He was also a tinker who owned a fleet of rag and bone carts pulled by ponies, which also belonged to him. He earned a decent living combining these two completely different businesses. Barry was about the same age as me and Peter was a couple of years younger. Barry was a strange mixture: handy with his fists, yet at the same time a rather sensitive soul. He later became a scenic artist for Yorkshire Television.

The head teacher was a local Conservative councillor and part of our 'curriculum' was to deliver political leaflets to houses and shops in the area. I wondered how my dad would have felt, had he known he had been working long hours in a mill in order to pay for me to help campaign for the Tories? I was only a young lad of 12, but already I could clearly see that this school thrived on gullible people like Mum and Dad, people who cared about their children's education, despite their offspring being far from the brightest marbles in the bag. The school also got us kids to write ready-prepared letters to various companies, begging for free produce, which was to be sold at our local charity event in the school. What that charity was I have no idea, though rumours abounded that it was probably the head of the establishment's political campaign. I couldn't bring myself to tell Mum and Dad about the realities of this place as I was certain Dad would have replied, 'What do you know, you're only a kid.'

In an attempt to deal with this dilemma, I became a class clown. We began writing 'The Works', which was an exercise book full of explanatory drawings, the whole object being to disrupt the class. Chair shuffling, desk lid dropping, collective humming and animal noises were just a few of our ploys that resulted in much disruption. One lad even brought a pet mouse to school and let it loose during maths, which caused a near riot: screaming, tears and laughter, delightful mayhem to a mischievous kid.

As I mentioned, I suffered with severe migraines as a child and one day I had to come out of school because I went almost fully blind in one eye. The blood seemed to drain from my head, which was then filled with awful pain. Home was two bus journeys away, about 8 miles, I suppose. I tried getting on a bus, but couldn't, as I was forced to turn away and vomit in the street. Eventually I got onto the next bus and rode all the way with my head pressed against the cold glass window, trying to gain some relief from the awful pain. What brought these migraines on I do not know, though I suspect it may have been due to the stress I was under when living a double life: playing the nice church boy at home while being a terror both on the streets and at school. I eventually did tell Mum and Dad about the realities of that school and they agreed that it was a waste of both time and money. Mum sometimes worked as a shorthand typist, but Dad didn't like her working. In those days it was considered a slight on his manhood – not being able to support his wife.

Dad was still working at Transparent Paper Mill, but he had been promoted to foreman, which meant higher wages, though he still worked six days a week. Dad could now get a mortgage so we moved into a house with a bathroom, which was luxury after life without one. We now lived on Rochdale Road, less than a quarter of a mile from Heap Bridge, in a Victorian terrace. This was a dream family home for Mum and Dad, but Clive had joined the navy as a boy sailor at just 16, which meant that the new extra bedroom saw little use. It had taken Mum and Dad so long to save up for a family home that my brother and I had nearly grown up. I was then left alone with my mostly silent father and religious mother, which meant that non-communication was the order of the day. Mum occasionally drilled my head with religion, whereas Dad ignored me completely, until one day he announced that I was going to start work alongside him at the mill. I was 15 years of age and my schooling was over. It was now time to enter the real world of work.

Meanwhile, Granddad came to live with us. He had been in the coal mines from when he was 13 years of age till he was 65, and then stayed on working above-ground for another five years. He was Dad's dad and I believe that when he died he left my father £1,000 and Uncle Albert £1,000. Two thousand pounds was all he had to show for fifty-seven years of hard toil. Mum and Dad prepared the sitting room for him. It had in it, amongst other things, a bed, an easy chair and a radio: it was nice and cosy. I would go in there and try to talk to him on occasion. It wasn't easy, as his faculties were failing and he also spoke in an incredibly broad Lancashire accent. He also used words I couldn't easily understand: thee and thy, and clod, the real meaning of which I still do not know. He told me once of how he had 'clod' a man into a canal for beating his dog. Granddad would go every day to the Seven Stars pub nearby and there he would enjoy his stout. 'It keeps yer reg'lar,' he would say whenever he got onto the subject.

There was a coal fire in his room and no matter how we banked it up in order to keep the room warm for him, he would always take pieces of coal off and leave them on the side of the hearth. He was so set in his frugal ways that he couldn't indulge himself in a roaring open fire, even towards the end of his days. He was with us for only six months or so before he finally drifted away in his sleep, his hard toiling days at an end. Down at Listerfield Youth Club Paddy Kerwan asked why I hadn't been in on Tuesday. I told him of how my grand-dad had died and all he had to say was, 'The dead bastard.' Compassion, I concluded, wasn't part of his emotional range.

2

All in a Day's Work

It is the first of all problems for a man to find out what kind of work he is to do in this universe.

Thomas Carlyle

My job was to stand at the end of a paper-tube-producing machine and catch the cardboard tubes as a circular saw severed them into correct lengths. I would also load them onto trollies and they were then taken away. This endlessly repetitive routine went on for eight hours a day right through the working week. There was a large clock in my eyeline, which I looked at about every ten minutes, willing the day to end. I hated it with a huge amount of passion. Dad would walk by on occasion, but this was yet another place where he could ignore me. He had been at this mill for twenty-one years when I started my working life there, and I just couldn't comprehend how on earth he could stand it. My workmates were a mixture of English, Polish and Ukrainian men working twelve-hour shifts most days of the week, even seven days a week in some cases, in order to provide better-quality lives for their growing children. I admired them all for their selflessness, including Dad, but I knew even then that I did not want to be like them. Nay, that I could not be like them.

At that nutty school I had got to know all kinds of kids from all kinds of different backgrounds and so I felt I had an education of sorts, though not an academic one. I had been wrenched from my friends, together with my natural working-class evolution, at 11 years old and felt there was now no way back. That school had nurtured an even stronger sense of rebellion in me. I felt certain I could not fit in with the factory setting my father had sadly accepted. Dad had studied calligraphy before the war and sometimes spent his lunch break painting beautifully lettered posters for the works club. He also painted pictures as a hobby. That was what Dad had been intending to do as a career, but then all the new advances in printing came along and calligraphy became obsolete. All of Dad's studying had been for nothing. He often went to the club, known locally as the Tranny, for a game of snooker, but he never once asked me to go with him. Mum, on the other hand, always wanted me to go with her to the village hall, when I was a little kid, where she would sometimes play piano for the pantos and concerts which were put on there. She even volunteered me and Barry Nicholson for one of the shows, for which we had to do a bit of a dance routine. I would really rather have been playing football, but I went along with it for Mum's sake. Significantly, when I realised that Widow Twanky was actually the vicar, the full mystery and magic of the theatre was suddenly revealed to me.

The Princess Ballroom (locally known as the Prinnie) in Bury was an amazing theatrical experience during the 1950s. I was 13 my first time there, and as I opened the door I heard the sound of Little Richard singing 'Good Golly Miss Molly', recorded on vinyl of course. It was truly unforgettable. There were only two fashions in those days – teddy-boy or boring. We were allowed in on Saturday afternoons at that age, though they didn't seem to do too much age checking in the evenings either, so, as the dancehall had a bar, my drinking started young.

Mick Whelan was my mentor as regards the fashion for 'Teds'. He wore a long black jacket with blue piping around the pockets and was also the first person I ever saw wearing denim jeans. Prior to this I had only ever seen jeans in American films. The girls would often wear tight-fitting skirts with their hair piled high and profusely lacquered to keep it in place. They also sometimes wore hooped skirts and when jiving we would get glimpses of stocking tops. For a young lad with raging hormones this was a mixture of heaven and hell. When our favourite jiving records were played, the dance floor would be bouncing, the skirts flying, the stocking tops putting in yet more appearances. For sheer theatrical spectacle, I don't think such scenes have ever been bettered.

The Princess Ballroom attracted many characters and one family of well-known 'stars' was the Ainsleys; Harold, known as 'Az', Joan, Royce, Janice and Paula. The whole family was very good-looking and all were blessed with great personalities. They were amongst the best jivers I had ever seen. Harold, the elder brother, possessed film star looks along the lines of Paul Newman or Steve McQueen, and Royce, the younger brother, was very good-looking in a boyish way, with big blue eyes and curly blonde hair, which meant that all the girls fancied him. This popularity with the female of the species compelled me to seek his company. Joan, the elder sister, was very sophisticated and elegant, though they came from the backstreets of Bury. In fact, there was something very showbiz about the whole family. I was quite good friends with Royce, in particular, for a time.

I eventually managed to grow little wispy sideburns and bought a second-hand long black jacket with a velvet collar from someone who slips my memory, for a pound, which was quite a sum in those days. I took to hiding this because if Dad had seen me wearing it he would have gone berserk. Perhaps because of this I drifted even further from my family and began hanging around with a bunch of local tough guys in the town centre.

According to popular opinion the best teddy boys came from the Elton area of Bury and among these lads were some real hard-cases. Looking older than my 16 years, I would get into pubs quite easily, where I would listen to the conversations always in full flow. Fights were common, usually between navvies and teddy boys.

Paddy Kerwan and Mick Dolan were considered the hardest teenagers in town and this made me want to get to know them better, so I began going to Listerfield Youth Club on a more regular basis. All the tough guys of Elton hung out there and it was there that I first met Hardy, real name David Morgan Hardman, who was a very colourful character. In my opinion, he was a full-blown lunatic, in fact, and was also a close friend of Paddy and Mick.

When I first saw him he was standing on a radiator peeping out from behind some curtains. Then he would suddenly leap out onto people's backs and frighten them half to death. It quickly became obvious that Paddy, Mick, Hardy and Mick 'Dougie' Douglas were a team. They were so close, in fact, that they pooled their money and had a sort of unwritten 'life and death' bond. They were quite a fearsome and impressive bunch to a young, impressionable mind like my own. True, they were all misfits from the rough end of town, but all were lovable rogues nevertheless. In fact, I felt it a privilege to be knocked on my backside during a youth club boxing match with 'Mighty' Mick Dolan. A strange way to feel, perhaps, but such a feeling was justified when Mick later became an ABA Light Heavyweight finalist. I had been in with a champ! He seriously loved his boxing, but he loved a street fight too. I once fought alongside him during a major dance hall barnie at the Winter Gardens in Blackpool.

My oddball humour seemed to compliment Hardy's personality and antics, and so we soon became the very best of friends. His twin brother had died after tragically drowning when they were small boys. Sadly, he didn't know who his father was, though he didn't seem to allow the past to hold him back, as he was very bright, with an inquisitive mind. He worked as a skilled sheet metal worker and was also the funniest (unofficial) street entertainer I have ever seen. Hardy would perform a surreal series of leaps and noises which bewildered and frightened folk around the town centre. He would suddenly go into mock fits and then leap to his feet just as people were approaching to help. He would also do pretend karate chops at passers-by, while shouting, 'Zip, zap, zip, zap,' so he became known as Mad Hardy.

His 'zip-zapping', as we called it, didn't endear him to everyone and occasionally his crazy antics ended in a fight when some offended member of the public retaliated. However, when he strung together such antics into a form of abstract street theatre, he would very soon have the watching crowd, myself among them, crying with hysterical laughter. I occasionally joined in his performances, but I was never as good as he was. He now lives in Holland, which means we don't see each other very often, but we remain close friends to this day. Of course, he has calmed down somewhat since those early days of our friendship, but he is still not averse to the odd 'zip-zap'.

Another good friendship from around the same time was with Kev Jackson, who was the lead singer with the Manchester band The Powerhouse 6, though his stage name was Kev Curtis. At just 17 years of age he was fronting one of Manchester's most popular rock bands. I just felt I had to get to know him. He was small in stature and full of energy, with a mass of copper-coloured curly hair. He had proven a popular guest act while on holiday at Butlin's holiday camp, where he was backed by Rory Storm's band, The Hurricanes, from Liverpool. Ringo Starr was the drummer, who would later become incredibly famous after joining The Beatles. Kev had a unique sense of humour, quite distinct in fact, and often made up what I believe are termed 'word salads'. He had a wide range of knowledge about music and he persuaded me to begin listening to jazz, which I had stayed well clear of before meeting him. Kev Jackson remains a close friend to this day.

Paddy Kirwan arranged a night out for us all in Manchester, at what were then known as strip and blue clubs. Strippers paraded and comics told racist, sexist, filthy jokes. There were around fifteen of us and we joined in the cheering of good-looking strippers and the jeering of those who were not quite the right weight, which was the custom in those times. The ticket price included a plate of meat and potato pie with red cabbage, which was served at the end of the night, the main focus being the strippers, the comics and the heavy drinking.

For some inexplicable reason I became separated from the rest of the lads, who were well ahead of me in the line for supper. So I decided to ask one of the lads to take my ticket and get my supper, as well as his own, so that I wouldn't miss the hired bus for the journey home. Whilst doing so, however, a lad in the line-up accused me of pushing in, but I explained that I was getting a mate to get my supper for me so that I didn't miss the bus home. As I lifted my arm to hand over the ticket the same chap pushed it back down. With a skinful of drink inside me, I decided the guy would need to be taught some manners and so I threw what was meant to be a left hook, but it missed. We ended up wrestling around the room until two bouncers finally grabbed us and clattered us out. My opponent then got in a few jabs, while I swung at him, but mostly missed. I tried to move in closer in order to get hold of him, while fending off a few more blows; then I put my head down and lunged at him. I got a firm hold on his lapels. Now it was my turn. I dragged him to the ground, only to hear Hardy shouting, 'Steve, Steve, it's me.'

Hardy had come out of the club to try and stop the fight by getting between us, but because I'd had my head down I had grabbed hold of the wrong person. We got to our feet and my opponent was gone, nowhere to be seen, no doubt enjoying a good chuckle at my expense. My nose had taken rather a pounding and was bloody and broken. It was already a bit flat, but was now well pummelled. I suppose I could have gone without supper, but I was hungry and needed something to eat, so had decided to pursue the matter. Was it worth it? Not really. True, I now had a rather amusing anecdote to dine out on, but laughter is very short-lived, while my broken nose is permanent!

For a village boy like myself, meeting all of these colourful characters was a really exciting experience. I'd met Kev Curtis, the singer; Ian Wallace, the drummer; and David Morgan Hardman, the nutter.

I had been working at Transparent Paper Mill for about eight months when my mother noticed an advertisement for a course that was due to begin at Bury Technical College, working towards GCE qualifications. I didn't particularly want to enrol on this course, but then again I had no desire to remain standing rooted to that blasted machine all day as it spewed out tube after tube after tube. And so, realising that I would need some skills to get on in the world, I quit the job and began the course. I was determined that I would really get my head down and work hard.

I did work hard when it came to art and English lessons, but my concentration fled during physics, maths and history, as these held very little interest for me. History was just too full of kings, queens and wars. Maybe I would have done better had the subjects been the Industrial Revolution, or the history of coal mining. Conventional school history had, I felt, no relevance to my life, or so it seemed at the time.

Only three of us studied art and classes were held at the little art school on Broad Street in Bury. Georgina was our teacher and she began teaching us about the Impressionists – Monet, Manet, Toulouse-Lautrec, Renoir and van Gogh being the main subjects. I admit to becoming fascinated with their lives and began hungrily devouring their biographies, which led to me wondering if I could become a successful artist. I felt that this would be a great way to live and concluded very quickly that Modigliani would never have settled for a life at Transparent Paper Mill. My year in college passed relatively quickly and I finished up with art and English O Levels, which, I could not help feeling, were going to be of very little use to me in the industrial north of England.

Several of my friends from Listerfield Youth Club were apprentice engineers, so I began to wonder if that was a career I should pursue. I acted quickly, applied for a job and got it: apprentice fitter at Webb's Forge. The wage was very poor, so I would have to rely on Dad's help with money. I thought this was the way ahead, but it didn't take long for me to realise that I had made a big mistake. All of the machines were the wrong way round, as I was left-handed in a right-handed world. This meant that I was out of place before I had even got started. Also, the forge was unbelievably noisy and hot. Webb's specialised in making massive crankshafts for ships and the hot metal was pounded into shape under huge steam hammers. It was deafening and the air stifling. I was often in there helping the fitters by passing them the right tools at the right time. My overalls would be ringing wet with sweat after a matter of seconds. It was hell in there.

Alan Roberts, another mate from the youth club, also worked at Webb's, in the turning shop, working on lathes. Alan and I shared an interest in silent movies and there was a re-run of these films on television at the time. And so I would go round to his house and we would sit rocking with laughter as we watched Harold Lloyd, Charlie Chaplin, Buster Keaton, and Laurel and Hardy. Tears would stream down our faces, we laughed that much at these old films. Alan was a very good footballer and he played semi-professionally for many years, before finally becoming a professional player. He later set up a successful carpet business in Bury and we still see each other occasionally.

We often went to the Bury Palais from work in our overalls, boots and donkey jackets, as it opened at lunchtime. This was a dance hall where lots of girls congregated and where I first met Susan, who, although only about 14 years of age, was already very beautiful. I would have been about 18 then and many of the girls would flirt with us older boys. One day, during a lunchtime visit there, I made a ring out of a piece of old newspaper and put it on Susan's finger, as though I was staking my claim on her for the future. By this time we had entered the early 1960s and the fashions had begun to change.

The teddy-boy haircuts had been combed down, the Brylcreem thrown out. Instead, hair was washed and all of us wanted to be either a Beatle or a Rolling Stone, though some, I think, would have settled for being a Trogg, an Animal or even a Kink! The Bury Palais was owned by a local bookmaker called Wally Wilson and we pestered and pestered him to get all of the top bands to play at his venue. In reply to our constant pestering, I can vividly remember him saying, 'I'm not going to pay for them, not The Who. No, not when you can book Herman's Hermits for a tenner.' Actually, The Who did eventually appear there, but we mostly had to travel up the valley, to Rawtenstall Astoria, which booked many of the best bands, including The Kinks, The Animals, Wayne Fontana and the Mindbenders, and The Hollies, all of which I saw perform.

I quickly realised that I would never make an engineer and this, coupled with the fact that I was always short of cash, made me quit my job at Webb's – I went to work at a local cotton mill instead. My duties were to weigh rolls of cloth removed from the looms and then record the weights in a book. This having been accomplished, I would transport the cotton rolls to the 'overlooker' and this, basically, amounted to my new career. Not much of a step up from the paper mill, true, though it wasn't quite as repetitive or draining, physically or mentally.

Work wasn't hard to find in those days as there was plenty about, particularly in industry, and most men seemed to be employed. In fact, the streets were distinctly devoid of men during daytime hours, as the vast majority found employment in one form or another. The town centre was always busy with women and young children not yet in school, and unemployed men, most anyway, were ashamed to be seen out of work, apart from a few villains who hung out in Colson's Café. A lot of tinkers and gypsies also gathered there, discussing their plans for their various scrap metal ventures. I occasionally took a day off work and went to Colson's Café in order to listen to them discussing their seemingly rich and varied lives, full of colour and character, while secretly wishing that I could be a part of it all.

Around that time Kev, Hardy and I read Jack Kerouac's soul-searching travelogue *On the Road*, which left a lasting impression on all of us. I began to feel that my destiny was maybe to be a beatnik poet, or possibly a rock star; I wasn't exactly sure which. And so I bought an old guitar and restrung it to suit left-handed playing. We then decided to form a band down at the youth club with Paddy Kirwan on drums, Dave Ogden on bass guitar and me on rhythm guitar with a single pick-up. I had learnt to play three chords, but hadn't a clue as to how to tune the instrument. Consequently the chords did all sound very similar. Nevertheless, undaunted, we went ahead with a performance at the youth club under our band name, The Saracens. I was duly sacked from the band after that one performance, the main reason being, I was told, because I was crap. I then bought a second-hand drum kit from Ian Wallace, who was leaving a band called The Jaguars in order to join The Warriors. He was a fabulous drummer and he was also left-handed, which was inspirational to me. Ian eventually hit the big time and moved to America, where he became a session drummer on, among other impressive projects, Bob Dylan's *Budokan*. He also became the drummer for the cult progressive rock band King Crimson and played for Jackson Browne and the Crimson Jazz Trio.

I practiced my drumming regularly and made such progress that I was eventually asked to take Ian Wallace's place in The Jaguars. We performed covers of blues and R&B numbers at Bury Palais, Bolton Palais, Manchester venues, and various pubs and clubs. My dad never gave anything away when he found out I was part of a band, but years later Mum told me that he had been quite impressed that I was actually being paid to play drums. Our success was limited though and so this, coupled with a lack of enthusiasm and the fact that there were so many bands around at the time, meant that we eventually disbanded. My thoughts drifted back to Kerouac's book and the life of the travelling beatnik. I then decided to save what money I could and after a few weeks I would set off 'on the road' in order to find adventure and freedom, and to see if that was what I wanted out of life.

I didn't want Mum and Dad to try to talk me out of this plan, so I just left a note telling them that I would be in touch and that I was on my way to London. I carried with me a little duffle bag, a sleeping bag and a few personal belongings, hitching lifts all the way to London. The first lift was with a chap who looked very much like a beatnik himself, with his scruffy hair and beard. He was driving a little old rusty van with bee hives in the back. After around twenty minutes or so we hit thick fog and I thought he would slow down, but he just kept on going, seemingly oblivious to the dangers ahead. Not only that, but some of the bees were escaping and they were now circling around our heads, though this didn't seem to bother him either. Eventually I felt compelled to ask him to 'Slow down you nutcase,' but he just replied, 'Whatever fate has in store, there is nothing we can do about it.' So he continued on through the fog, completely blind to any danger ahead, such as a build-up of traffic. Boy was I glad to get out of that van. Some of his bees were equally glad, it seemed, as quite a few of them disembarked when I did.

I can't remember much about the others who offered lifts that day: it was such a long time ago. But I did get to London before nightfall, which was a city I had never before visited. I knew of many of the famous landmarks, of course, so I was fascinated as I saw them in real life for the very first time – Shaftsbury Avenue, Oxford Circus, Buckingham Palace, the River Thames, the Southbank and, not least among them, Trafalgar Square – where about seven beatniks were gathered, some of whom I got to know quite well. They began to teach me how to survive on virtually no money at all, such as taking the milk and bread that was often left outside cafes in the early mornings. I justified this in my mind by believing we were only eating what would have been thrown away anyway – this was probably not true, though there is no way of knowing.

I went to London during the summer months and so sleeping rough wasn't too bad at all. During the winter, the 'beats' would find empty buildings and sleep in there, out of the worst of the weather. This was before I had even heard of the word 'squatting'. I also spent many nights sleeping in the sitting position at Waterloo Station: if the police saw you lying down they would assume you were a vagrant and ask you to move on.

Daytime hours were spent in libraries or art galleries. It was at such places that I began writing what I thought at the time was deep spiritual poetry, though, looking back, I am sure these efforts were all rubbish. I think I have always held a belief in destiny and so I was constantly looking for signs that would hopefully put me on the right path. Although I was enjoying the feeling of being on the outside of mainstream society, the money I had saved was fast disappearing and I was not enjoying the hunger I felt.

One of the beatniks I met was nicknamed Posh Peter, a man who had been adopted by a rich family as a baby and sent to a public school. After trying to find his place in the world, and failing, he had decided to drop out of society altogether and was now about to hitch a lift down to Kent for the hop-picking season. I thought I would join him. We went into a library and picked out a village near Faversham where he knew hop-picking was in progress. We would hitch lifts separately and then we would meet up at the village we had settled on. It took me two days to reach that village and I spent a night sleeping in a field.

When I finally arrived, at around midday, I saw Peter sitting on a park bench, reading an old newspaper upside down, for some strange reason. I didn't question it. We then set off, wandering along the long country lanes, calling at farm after farm after farm and enquiring about available work in the area. Unfortunately for us, gypsies and other travellers had beaten us to it. We sat on a nearby bench next to a bus stop, close to despair. By now we were both starving hungry and without money; the life of the beats may have been feeding my soul, but it certainly wasn't feeding my belly. As soon as it went dark we tried to get to sleep in a nearby field, as there was nothing else to do.

Next morning we ate apples from orchards as we passed along the lanes, as hunger pangs were becoming more dominant in my mind than anything else. However, I was learning that it is possible to be in a state of permanent hunger and still survive, as many poor people in the world are forced to do each day. During the Kent wanderings with Posh Peter I took some food from a bird table in someone's garden and that bread tasted unbelievably good; so good, in fact, that I cannot begin to describe the experience. Years later I read *The Life of Buddha* and realised that this self-inflicted rejection of the material world was a well-trodden path for people trying to discover a deeper meaning to their existence. Buddha was a privileged prince who gave up everything for a life of poverty. Some would call that madness, but I wouldn't, as I could see that the endless pursuit of wealth seemed to cause so much unhappiness in the world.

Peter knocked on the door of a large detached house and asked for water, as it was a very hot day. A kindly old lady brought us a jug of iced tea, which I had never tasted before, and then she said, 'Are you boys hungry?' The cheese and spring onion sandwiches that followed were adorable.

We then decided to try to jump on a train back to London without being seen; this was easily done, as the little village station was deserted. Once aboard, we continually changed carriages and moved around in order to avoid the ticket collector, which we succeeded in doing, and eventually arrived back at Waterloo. We sneaked off, crossed the tracks and exited through a nearby gate. Peter was barefoot, as he had no shoes, nor did he own a sleeping bag. All he seemed to have was an old boiler suit, which he used for sleeping in. I too was soon to be barefoot, as my 'Jesus sandals' disappeared one afternoon as I slumbered in the sun outside the National Gallery.

Later on a few of us decided we would try hitching across London to Richmond for the Jazz and Blues Festival. Three of us made it – Posh Peter, me and another guy, who was inexplicably called Peldon Treem. We found a way through the fencing and got into the arena. And there, standing before us on stage, were the Rolling Stones. It must have been only just after the success of their first album, as they were not yet top of the bill.

Whilst in Richmond I caught sight of myself in a shop window and was shocked at how thin I was, with long hair down my back and a thick beard covering much of my face. I thought at the time that I looked like some sort of lunatic apostle. When I look back it seemed as though there was some sort of a guardian of the beatniks, as, despite our life of deprivation, we were still able to travel around the country, and all for free. Back in London an amazing thing happened. I was engaging in the sit-up and sleep position at Waterloo when I suddenly opened my eyes and caught sight of my brother in the distance dressed in his navy uniform. He had obviously been on leave in Bury and was heading back to Portsmouth. He failed to recognise me when I first shouted over because of the long hair and beard, but then it suddenly dawned on him who I was. We exchanged hugs and handshakes before he was forced to catch his train, and thankfully he gave me a few quid before we parted. I felt sad, as well as envious, for Clive had a purpose in life and as yet I didn't. I still had no idea in which direction my life would go.

My situation was now getting desperate and I was forced to beg for money. Whenever I did get a bit of cash together I would write home and tell Mum and Dad that I was fine and for them not to worry. Mum would sometimes send me a little cash, care of the Trafalgar Square Post Office. What I was doing in London, leading such a life, I still do not know, even today. I suppose it was a kind of mental aberration, or maybe one might call it romantic naivety. I continued on, surviving as best I could. One night three or four of us were attempting to get some sleep on park benches near Charing Cross station when a policeman approached and told us to move on. He took our names and warned us that if he had to move us on again during the night, or any other night he might come across us, we would all be arrested.

A few nights later we found that a door had been left open at an old deserted government building and decided we would sleep in there, where it seemed to be warm and safe, but at around four o'clock in the morning the police came bursting through the doors with loud barking dogs. We were all arrested, though nobody was having sex, taking drugs or doing anything illegal as far as we knew. We were homeless and none of us had any money, so it seems it was a crime to seek safe shelter. We spent some time in the cells and were eventually charged with wandering abroad, under the Vagrancy Act. Sentencing would not take place for another two weeks and so, ironically, I was taken back to Kent, where I was held in the Ashford Remand Prison. Again, it was a free ride.

I was able to shave my beard, have a haircut, a bath and was given clean prison clothes and enjoyed 'food-heaven'. However, I dreaded writing home to Mum and Dad because I knew the situation I now found myself in would depress them, which is odd, in a way, because I wasn't in the least bit depressed. I was clean, warm and well fed, which allayed any potential depression due to my confinement. With two weeks of regular eating behind me, I got yet another free ride back to London and went to court. I was put on probation under the condition that I returned home. Dad was reluctant to have me back, but Mum had persuaded him that it was the best thing for me under the circumstances, so they had posted me money for my journey home. Otherwise I would have been sent to a probation hostel.

During the long and tedious coach ride back to my old life, I tried to gather my thoughts and make some sense of what the life of the travelling beatnik was all about. The nearest I could get to making any sense of it at all was that it was quite natural for a young man to want to fly the nest, even if I was attempting to do that in a rather unconventional way. My instincts told me to go out into the big wide world and make a life for myself, but on reflection I was poorly equipped for such a move. I was a romantic dreamer and found it difficult to survive in a capitalist society. Artists of any kind, whether they be actors, writers, poets, painters or musicians, have to be at the top of their game in order to make a living at what they do best. I was an average painter. Though I could play the drums, I was no expert, and my poetry was chronic. How on earth would I ever be able to make a living?

Along the way I also wondered what Mum and Dad's reaction was going to be when I saw them. I think Dad would have been happy if I could have been a professional sportsman, such as a footballer or boxer. Mum, on the other hand, would never have been happy, as I had failed her from day one by not being the daughter she had always wanted. The next best thing I could have done for Mum would have been to have become a gay vicar who would look after her in old age. One thing is for certain; neither of them wanted a manic-depressive hobo for a son.

I eventually arrived home and seeing Mum and Dad again made me feel terrible. Not only was I a failure, but I now had a criminal record too, though I was hardly Al Capone. I soon settled down again and found a job at another cotton mill. It was as if I had never been away. Susan, the girl I had met at Bury Palais and to whom I had given that paper ring, was older now and we met up again and began going out together, though not on a regular basis. If I had been a tradesman such as an electrician, bricklayer or joiner, I could have earned some decent money and begun thinking seriously about my future, such as getting married or buying a house. But as things stood I was poorly paid and had also developed a drink problem. I didn't drink at all while I was in London, or on my travels elsewhere, probably because I never had enough money to eat properly, let alone drink alcohol. But I now had a job, and as boring as it was, it meant that I could afford to drink. In fact, the only excitement I could get in my life was going down to the pub at the weekend.

Friday and Saturday nights invariably ended with me staggering or crawling on my hands and knees through the park opposite our house because, without exception, I drank far too much and always ended up bladdered. I would sometimes be sick in the park and try to sleep it off on a bench there, before finally going into the house, just in case Mum or Dad saw the state I was in. I didn't consider this to be a form of alcoholism, as everybody seemed to drink too much in those days, just as most young ones today often drink too much at weekends. I wasn't painting or writing poetry at that time, but I believe I was attempting to live the hedonistic lifestyle of a successful creative artist. The problem was, I wasn't creating anything at all; well, nothing more than severe, chronic hangovers.

3

A Different Challenge

Discipline is learnt in the school of adversity.
Mahatma Gandhi

I think it was around this time that the famous Twisted Wheel Club opened in Manchester, which became an obsession for me and many others. I was fortunate enough to see several great bands at this club, including The Spencer Davis Group with the young Stevie Winwood, Georgie Fame, Screamin' Jay Hawkins, Long John Baldry with Rod Stewart, Brian Auger and the Trinity, and, best of all, The Graham Bond Organisation, whose members, would later form the legendary group Cream. We would stand transfixed as we watched the complex rhythms being played by Ginger Baker, the drummer, on his classic Ludwig kit. One night we noticed that Charlie

Watts of the Rolling Stones was also transfixed by the masterful drumming of Ginger Baker. I approached and asked Mr Watts for a light for my cigarette just so that I could say hello.

During those early days the Twisted Wheel Club was very much a place suited to beatniks and the like, but after only a year or so, the mod phenomenon began and fashions very quickly changed, resulting in beards being shaved off, hair being cut and brogue shoes being worn. The young working classes were becoming more affluent and they wanted to show it off. The music even began to change, moving away from blues and R&B. Soul music was becoming ever more popular. Ray Charles, The Four Tops, The Temptations, The Drifters, The Isley Brothers, Jan and Dean, Stevie Wonder and Percy Sledge being just a few of the best pioneers of soul music. I must confess that I was saddened to see the end of the beatnik era as I felt that such a lifestyle was more me. I adapted to the change in the end, shaving off my beard and having a mod haircut, and I began wearing a suit.

I also began listening to jazz music. Some of my favourite artists were Miles Davis, Dave Brubeck, Jimmy Smith and Wes Montgomery. After watching Ginger Baker and seeing some of the great jazz drummers on TV, I realised there was little, if any, point in me taking up drumming again, as I knew that I would have to practice hard every day probably for several years if I was ever to succeed in emulating those legendary musicians. During the start of the mod era, drugs became more popular and the most used were purple hearts and other amphetamines, which would keep those who used them awake all night. Fortunately I wasn't attracted to this lifestyle, thank goodness, as I had enough problems with the drink.

Mick Douglas was the first person I knew to become a mod. He was a welder and he could earn very good money, sometimes working abroad, in places such as Saudi Arabia. Thus he could afford expensive clothes. The rest of us just tried to follow his lead. Dougy, as he was known to his friends, also introduced us to several new artists. One of these was Mose Allison, the great blues singer, who was a big influence on Georgie Fame. Another great singer was Sugar Pie DeSanto. A young lad named André hung around with us at that time and he and his older brother, Steph, were very much a part of the local mod scene. We would take André to the Twisted Wheel Club, which helped shape his lifelong passion for music. He later amassed a huge collection of records and I heard that he sometimes organises and DJs at soul nights. He was only 15 when we first began taking him to the nightclub to see various bands. Sadly, I have seen nothing of him for many years.

I usually went into Manchester every Saturday night, to the Wheel, but one week a small circus visited Bury and I decided I would go and see the show, which was a family-run affair. Most of the lads I regularly knocked about with thought I had gone off my head and they weren't shy about telling me, but I had always had a fascination with the circus and so I went along, despite the mickey-taking. I am glad I did as, lo and behold, who should appear as Etna the Fire Eater but Keith Smith, the Wonder Boy of Heywood. He also appeared as a clown during the evening's entertainment. I do not know what happened to Keith, though I do hope he remains in show business to this day. Seeing him again started me off thinking about the joy to be had from performing for a crowd and I realised that I very much missed the high I got from playing in a band.

I eventually fell out with the mod scene as it was a bit too elitist for my taste. I grew my beard again by way of rebellion. I also began reading more and Dostoevsky, Balzac, and Albert Camus' *The Outsider* graced my bookshelf. Well at least till I had to take them back to the library, that is. I was attempting to find a role model, but nothing would gel. This led to yet more heavy drinking. I found little in life to be positive about, except, perhaps, the buzz I got from downing pint after pint of a weekend. I was in a rut and couldn't see a way out, but one night something happened which would eventually change my life forever.

A gang of us were all wandering home, very drunk and wishing that we could carry on drinking, but in those days, eleven o'clock in the evening was closing time at the pubs and so we headed for home, walking, or should I say staggering, up The Rock in Bury, towards an area known as Moorgate. Along the way we noticed an off-licence and displayed in the window were bottles of whisky, wine, gin, rum and a whole lot more. I cannot remember who threw the brick, but before we knew it the window was smashed and away we all ran with the stolen booze. The decision to grow my beard again proved a bad one, as someone reported the incident to the police, saying that a bearded youth was among a gang of lads who had run away from the scene of the smashed window. Eric Wilson's flat was nearby and we headed there, but the police caught us very quickly. Some of the lads managed to get away, but, fitting the bill of the 'bearded youth', I was quickly caught and held, which meant that I ended up taking the rap for us all. I was still on probation after my escapades in London, so things looked bleak. I appeared in court soon after and the judge decided I needed a short, sharp shock and sentenced me to three months in Buckley Hall Detention Centre.

In my drunken stupidity I had hurt Mum and Dad yet again, and I felt terrible. Yet even during these low periods in my life I managed to somehow look forward to a new experience, possibly because I was still searching for something that would make at least some sense of my life. Detention centres in those days were run on very similar lines to the army and discipline was tough. It was 'Yes sir, no sir' at all times and my kit had to be laid out every morning for inspection before morning parade. I spent the first few days scrubbing floors and one morning while I was busy doing this a prison officer came over and said, 'I want a word with you, lad.'

'Yes sir,' I replied and he led me off to a nearby classroom and then drew a swastika on the blackboard with a broken piece of chalk.

'What do you think that means lad?' he asked.

'I don't know sir.'

He then began explaining what it meant, but I couldn't take in what he was saying and my mind just drifted off. All I could think was, 'This man's a Nazi.' Then the same screw stopped me another day and said, 'There's a job for you in the kitchen.' For some reason I had been given what was considered a 'soft' job, though I didn't know the reason for having been shown favour in this way.

The kitchen staff had to be up earlier than the other inmates in order to make cocoa and to make a start on preparing breakfast for everyone. The rest of the lads would be running around the yard in their shorts at seven o'clock in the morning, which had been my fate until I was given that job in the kitchen. The very first time I ladled cocoa out through the small hatch, I felt a knife sticking into my lower back. It was held by a trustee who was due to be let out in a week's time. Whenever certain lads came for their cocoa – those he didn't like – he would push the knife into my back and say, 'Burn, burn.' To my horror, I was forced to pour boiling hot cocoa over the hands of complete strangers, as I couldn't be sure if this lunatic would stab me if I didn't. I desperately attempted to indicate that the guy behind me was responsible, but I failed to get my silent message across to the victims. I burnt four lads in that cocoa-scalding session, but fortunately I was able to explain to them later on what had really occurred and, thankfully, they believed me as this psycho was a sworn enemy and his antics were not unknown.

My legs nearly collapsed under me as I ran to the shower after completing my first stint of circuit training, which, although part of the 'new experience' I was seeking, made me realise that it wasn't going to be easy by any stretch of the imagination.

Not least because we were expected to continually improve on our circuit training times. We were timed and different coloured sashes were given according to the times we achieved. All of this was to build remission time so that you didn't have to serve your full sentence. The lad who did the fastest circuit was chalked up in the gym and this, always without exception, read 805 Smith; he was the 'Daddie' in there.

We also attended classes in the evenings and these were a matter of personal choice. I chose woodwork and art. In the art class I was working on a painting which was shaping up really well, but one evening someone, possibly because they deemed my work to be too good, daubed paint all over it. Perhaps jealousy had been the motive behind this act of vandalism; I do not know, but weeks of work were ruined by that one cruel act. Perhaps it was karmic repayment for the damage to the off-licence.

During morning parade we had to stand to attention and a particular screw always stopped when he reached me and said, 'Have you not shaved this morning, boyo?'

I would always reply, 'Kitchen staff, sir; excused shaving, sir, until after parade.' Then he would try to pull hairs from my face while I stood to attention, which was very irritating, but we just had to put up with such strange behaviour from our so-called superiors as retaliation would have brought nothing but more trouble.

We slept in long dormitories and, thankfully, we did have a chance to do some reading before lights out. There was a small library at the detention centre and to my surprise I came across a book by Jean-Paul Sartre, so I began studying existentialism. The floor of the dormitory was highly polished and thus slippery, so one evening, in an attempt to find some sort of freedom in this restricted environment, I purposely slipped and fell. The screw standing nearby laughed mockingly, as did several of the inmates, but I felt I was in full control of the situation and was laughing inside because I had fallen on purpose.

At mealtimes we were forbidden to speak, and if anyone uttered even a word they would be punished – this is just one example of the restricted environment we were in. This suppression led to at least one person, every day, doing bunny-hops around the canteen. Sometimes a little bunny-hopping convoy would be circling the room as we enjoyed egg and chips, dry bread, and tea with no sugar.

During woodwork classes I carved a wooden head and stand from a single piece of wood and I was pleased with the finished article, even though it was rather primative to say the least, so I asked if I could change classes. I wasn't sure of the reaction I would get, but they agreed and I chose drama instead. I enjoyed these classes a lot and the sound of hard-case lads from Liverpool, Manchester and Newcastle reading the female parts from Oscar Wilde's *The Importance of Being Earnest* was hysterical.

As the weeks passed I grew more and more familiar with the routine, which was becoming easier with time. I could do my kit without any problems. I was improving on my circuit times and was getting stronger and fitter by the day. To bed early, up early in the morning, regular exercise, three basic meals a day, coupled with no smoking or drinking and no sugar did me the world of good. Every young lad who entered the detention centre overweight was soon fit and slim, and every young man who was skinny quickly put weight on. The life inside – the diet, the strict rules, the daily routine – was geared to producing healthy, fit and disciplined young men who would be better prepared for life on the outside, back among society.

Playing football also improved my fitness and I was quite a good left-winger. One Saturday morning all who wanted a game were allowed and we played a full ninety minutes so that the screws could pick out a team for the afternoon. I was picked to play left-wing, against a decent amateur cup-winning team from Manchester and the screw in charge of us, who was also in the team, said, 'We're not going to win easily, so get stuck in.' That was really an unofficial way of instructing us to kick them off the field. This was reinforced when he concluded his pre-match banter with a nod and a wink.

We did get stuck in and during the match I leapt into the air as I challenged for a header. I heard the whistle blow and wondered what had happened. And then I saw the lad I had challenged lying on the floor with a bloody nose. I was baffled, as I hadn't even felt any contact with him. However, no one else had been involved so it had to have been my fault. I must have elbowed him in the face. Our coach, the screw, obviously didn't believe it was an accident, as he came over and winked at me, whispering, 'Well done.' It seemed strange that such perceived dirty tactics were acceptable. It was as though the coach wanted it to have been done on purpose, even though many of the inmates would have been sent there for similar violence on the outside. What a contradictory society we live in, don't you think?

I was experiencing a new vigour which, at times, could be very frustrating. As I stood on parade every day, looking up at the mysteries of the sky, I often wanted to shout out just for the sheer mad joy of being alive. But of course, inside, that would have been a punishable offence. Unfortunately, this crazy energy burst out at the wrong moment, when we were about to go into a class. We were all standing in enforced silence, a long line of grey-trousered lads waiting for a blue-trousered screw to signal that it was time to move. It all seemed bonkers to me. I felt the tension in me rising, the pressure unbearable. I just wanted to shout, to move, to be free. I knew, of course, that rules and regulations and orderliness were essential, even valuable, in society. Yet I still could not channel my energy into something which was socially acceptable. I was holding my breath when the clock loudly announced the eighth hour, at which the screw began jangling his keys as he located the correct one and inserted it into the lock of the classroom door.

'In you go, you shitters,' he shouted, and an irresistible force compelled me to imitate him.

'In you go, you shitters,' I bellowed at top note, unable to stop myself. This, of course, led to punishment.

I was taken down to the gym, propelled forwards by sharp slaps to the back of my head. I was then forced to run around the gym with the screw throwing a large medicine ball at me, which I had to catch and throw back whilst still running. Although it was knackering, I was by this time very fit indeed and I could see that he was going to tire before I did. So I decided to spare him the embarrassment and myself future trouble by puffing and blowing and feigning exhaustion. I began pleading with him to stop, telling him that my arms were killing me. Eventually he ordered me back to the classroom in terms which many would consider unprintable, but I nearly burst out laughing right in his face. I just managed to stop myself in time. So the both of us, pink-faced and sweaty, went back to the classroom. It all seemed so hysterically and hopelessly insane that I wanted to shout, 'Get in, you shitbags,' just to see what would happen, but I managed to resist.

Sometimes all of us were taken down to the gym and we were made to play 'murder ball' in order to let off steam. Half the boys stood at one end of the gym and half stood at the other end; then a medicine ball was placed in the middle of the floor. There were no rules to this game – you just sort of made them up as you went along, though there was an objective. This was simply to get the medicine ball past the opposing team and to the opposite wall. I am sure you can imagine the pandemonium that broke out once the whistle had been blown. Grievances built up inside, so this game became an opportunity for scores to be settled. Many fights broke out as a result of this and the game often erupted into complete madness. I attempted to keep clear of all this by remaining on the periphery and hoping for a chance to seize the ball when no one else was interested. The trouble was every time I went for it someone would always jump on my back. The game would finish after about half an hour with the score always being a tedious nil–nil. I don't think the ball ever moved more than a few feet during the entire match, but a lot of injuries were sustained. I myself suffered a badly bruised back during one of these contests.

During the morning when a boy was due to be released we would serve breakfast to him. One morning I brought egg, bacon and beans to a ginger-haired lad named McFee, who had lost all his remission and had been forced to serve his full three-month term, but was now at last being set free. He had been on punishment almost every day for smoking, answering screws back and any number of other crimes. I lost count of the times I saw him running up and down stairs with a medicine ball on his head and hearing a screw shouting, 'AGAIN.' I said to him that it was all over now, and that he would have no more of this place. I thought he would be overjoyed, but he looked up at me with sad eyes and said that he was going to miss all his mates. This led me to wonder what sort of awful life he lived on the outside, though I had come to understand the camaraderie that builds in places like that. It could be very heart-warming so, to some extent, I understood how he felt.

The chef, who was also a screw, would never bother learning the names of the inmates he worked with, as, after a few weeks, they would be released and he would have to start all over again. So I was Lofty and another lad was known to him as Tubby. He wasn't fat: he just had a very round face, which gave the appearance of fatness. Tubby just couldn't seem to stop talking and this often got him into trouble. One day the screw who always attempted to pick hairs from my chin wandered into the kitchen while we were preparing dinner. We turned to look at him and for some unknown reason he said, 'A touch of the old how's your father, eh?'

Instead of keeping quiet Tubby said, 'What do you mean, sir? How's your father, sir?'

'Don't you f****** ask about my father, you lump. Don't ever mention his name,' said the screw. 'Get outside.' He then made Tubby do bunny-hops around the canteen and we could only conclude that the man was insane.

It hadn't dawned on me that I would be spending Christmas Day inside, but there were some perks associated with this, such as having more recreation time, when we played draughts, chess or dominoes. Of course, being a kitchen worker I helped prepare Christmas dinner. The usual traditions were kept up, though I think we served chicken rather than turkey. After the meal was over one of the screws got to his feet and formally announced that it was a tradition that any of the inmates who wished to entertain the assembled company could get up and do so now. One lad who imagined he was a stand-up comedian volunteered himself and told a few jokes, none of which were in the slightest bit funny. Despite this though, people began laughing at him (rather than with him!). He forgot the punch line to every joke he told and this became hysterical. Another lad got up and sang, doing an Elvis Presley impression: curled lip, wobbly legs, the whole package, in fact, and it was then that I noticed one of the prison officers looking at him with complete disdain, even contempt. Not an Elvis fan, I thought.

Even on Christmas Day it seemed that punishment was still dished out, as I noticed one lad doing bunny-hops around the canteen, but I had no idea what his crime had been. The prison officer not only made him do bunny-hops, but also made him put his arms round through his legs and reach to his ears. This meant that he was hopping around the room while holding onto his ears, which would have been very funny had some of the screws not derived such pleasure from forcing humiliating acts on the inmates. One lad got to his feet and announced that he wanted to tell a story and then began relating some tale that had happened to his family. He then got sidetracked onto another subject, which then led to yet another tale. This became so confusing that nobody, not even the teller of the tale himself, had any idea what he was jabbering on about. Eventually, and much to the relief of all sufferers, the screw took him by the elbow and led him back to his seat. I was thinking, sadly, about Susan and I began to wonder if she had found a new boyfriend, as we had been seeing one another on and off for a while before I got locked up. I wondered what she would be doing for Christmas.

I received a letter from Mum and she told me that Dad's health was gradually getting worse (he had a heart condition) and that he was going to have to stop work at the paper mill, on doctor's orders. Dad had paid towards his pension throughout his long working life and had even made contributions to a superannuation scheme, in order to top up his state pension, but the small print said he would lose half the money if he left the mill before reaching 65. That pension scheme, as has been the case in more recent times, was a complete stitch-up, and so Mum and Dad were left short. He was 61 at the time.

Mum had noticed, in one of her church magazines, an advertisement for an odd-job and security man at Burghley House in Stamford, Lincolnshire. The mill gave Dad impeccable references for his twenty-two years of service and undoubtedly it was such references that got him the job. This meant that he could semi-retire to a beautiful part of the country and there forget about his years in the mill. Mum was writing to tell me about this because, by the time I would be released, they would have moved.

I would like to think not, but I often wondered if the shame of his son being locked up had contributed in some measure to his deteriorating health. I guess I will never know one way or the other, though he was a very proud man and I imagine that such a thing could have affected him badly. As far as I was concerned, I just thought of my sentence as being the equivalent of National Service. Having gone through such things, I believe that today there should be some government-funded scheme to teach discipline and self-control to youngsters. Not necessarily to teach them how to fire guns, but to teach them how to interact properly with their fellow human beings. Although there were some lunatics among them, I have to say that most of the prison officers were good, honest, decent men who seemed to want to help us make the best of it while we were in there.

Circuit training, for some, would be conducted after lunch and the exertions would sometimes lead to one or two lads being sick, but they were forced to carry on and to clean it up after they had finished. This was hard on genuine cases of sickness, but an old screw told me they forced the lads to do this because some of the crafty guys would go into the gym with a mouthful of food and pretend to be sick just to get out of the training.

Occasionally one of the lads would suddenly appear sporting a black eye or a bust lip and of course the reason for such injuries was always that they had 'bumped into a door', because it was traditionally agreed among the inmates not to grass on anyone. One lad, a known malingerer, had managed to get himself a nice rest in hospital by wearing wet socks over a period of time, which eventually resulted in him getting an infection between his toes. On the morning that he came out of hospital we were all lining up ready to go on parade when 805 Smith sidled over to him and, unseen by the prison officers, stamped very hard on the malingerer's infected foot. I could see tears in his eyes from the severe pain and the frustration of being unable to call for help, as 'grassing' on 805 Smith could have been the most dangerous thing he could have done in his life.

I began wondering if I could keep up such a disciplined life once I was released. I was certainly fitter than at any time previous to this. This was obviously due to the regular exercise which was forced on us, but our diet was quite healthy too. No sugar was allowed and the food we ate contained very little fat. This diet, in fact, must have been very well balanced to have aided in producing such a fit and healthy bunch of young men. I couldn't smoke or drink inside, which obviously did me the world of good. Of all the things I missed, I think not seeing girls was the hardest to take. As regards all the other temptations on the outside, however, I think, in some ways at least, we would all be better off without them.

I soon realised just how 'conditioned' I had become while in the detention centre – if I saw beds not made properly, or kits not laid out correctly, it irritated me. Being orderly and disciplined doesn't come naturally, but needs to be imposed over a period of time to have any real effect, and I could now see clearly the value of it. Imposed discipline is one thing, but self-discipline is quite another, being much harder to achieve. I suspected that a lot of the prison officers had at one time been in the army and that they had found the lack of order and discipline in everyday civilian life difficult to cope with. Perhaps that is why they had chosen the careers they did?

For a change, I had done everything right during my incarceration and so gained full remission, which meant that the day finally came, after ten weeks, when I was served my last breakfast on the inside. I stood in line with two other lads, dressed in our civilian clothes, waiting to see the prison governor, who was holding our train passes. The screw who always tormented me walked past and got right in my face. 'Ah!' he exclaimed. 'Leaving us, are you, boyo?'

'Yes, sir,' I replied.

'Well don't f****** come back,' he yelled, slapping me very hard across the face. Even though I was tempted to butt him to the deck, I refrained, because if I had, I would almost certainly have gone straight to Borstal for three years for assaulting a prison officer. Anyway, I soon realised that it wasn't personal, as he also slapped the other two lads equally hard across their faces.

I felt a rising warm glow inside (and one on my cheek), as at last I walked to freedom. When I reached the railway station, the guard looked at my pass and said, 'Stamford, Lincolnshire, eh?'

'Yes, sir,' was my reply, and immediately I realised it was going to take me some time before I could stop saying 'sir' to people in uniforms.

4

Sea, Sun and Fun

Laughter is the shortest distance between two people.
Victor Borge

There was no direct train to Stamford, so I had to disembark at
Peterborough and then continue my journey by bus. Stamford,
as anyone who has been there will know, is a beautiful small
town – in stark contrast to the dark and grimy backstreets
of industrial Bury. In her letter Mum had told me to look for
Burghley House once I had reached Stamford, and then follow
her directions to where they were now living. As I passed
through the wide open spaces of the park, the stately home of
Burghley came into view. It almost took my breath away when
I realised that this was where Mum and Dad were living. I felt
I had landed on my feet!

I followed the directions written from Mum's letter and soon reached a gate with *Private* written on it. She had said to go through the gate, over a bridge and up a hill, and there it was: the farm where they lived, which looked as though it had come right out of a scene from *All Creatures Great and Small*. The wooden outbuilding had been adapted into a bungalow and that was where my parents resided. It was surrounded by a flock of sheep. When the door opened Mum gave me a hug and Dad just threw me a rather surly look. I had only been there a couple of hours, trying to make conversation, when Dad said, 'Right, I'm off to work.' Then he was away, out the door and walking down the road. I asked Mum where he was going at this time of night (it was seven o'clock in the evening) and she replied that he was on the night shift for the next twelve hours. Part of his job was to act as a security guard at Burghley House and so he had to check windows, doors and locks, etc., right through till morning.

Later that evening I strolled down to where Dad was, in a little office which the tourists used for purchasing tickets. There he sat, smoking away and reading the paper; very much the image I had always carried of him. I did manage to engage him in a little light conversation by asking him what his duties were. Amongst other things, he told me that on one particular day he'd had to open the gates leading to the main front entrance for an unnamed special visitor. As the rear window of the Bentley went down Dad was given a tip, a ten shilling note. By whom? – Paul Getty, one of the richest men in the world at that time.

Back at the bungalow Mum told me that they were worried Dad's job may be jeopardised if his employers discovered that I had been in a detention centre. I didn't want to admit it to myself, but deep inside I knew she was telling me in the gentlest way possible that they wanted me to get lost. I stayed with them for another couple of days to help Dad in the garden, which he was cultivating from a piece of spare land close to their home. Dad was wrestling with a big rock he was trying to move, which was obviously hampering progress, so I jumped in as fast as I could and shifted it for him single-handedly. Maybe I imagined it, but the expression on his face seemed to betray the fact that he was impressed, if only a little. Maybe Dad was surprised by what my stint at Buckley Hall had done for me, in a physical way at least.

Going from Buckley Hall to Burghley House in a single day was certainly a culture shock and I could not help but wonder what on earth my life was all about. I had always had a strong feeling of destiny – that there was something I was born to do – but it seemed to be becoming more and more unclear as to what that would be. I was confused and didn't know what to do. I did have a little money on me, from before I was sentenced, which would get me to goodness knows where. I decided to stay yet another day and walked around the more private areas of the estate. I walked right into the heart of the woodlands and there took off all my clothes, wandering around as though I was the first man, Adam. But, sadly, there was no Eve. It was my way of asserting and reclaiming my freedom from the constraints of the nick. However, there was a gamekeeper and no doubt this part of my story would have been much more amusing (to the reader, not necessarily me) if he had stumbled across me as I wandered around in the nude. Thankfully, he didn't.

The next day Dad went off to do his dayshift and he left a bit of money on the table for me as a farewell present. I said goodbye to Mum and asked her to thank Dad and say goodbye to him for me. Then I was off, dreaming of going to London, perhaps, or what about Paris? Possibly even Rome, or some other romantic and exotic destination. Instead, due more to Hobson's choice, because of my financial situation, I headed back to Bury, with its industry, its smoke and smog, its down-to-earth no-nonsense people. Why? Simply because I knew for certain that I had good mates there who would stand by me in times of trouble, want or need. My old mates would be there and I couldn't wait to see them. And, not least of all, Susan would be there.

I managed to get a job at a scenery hire studio at a place called Haslingden in the Rossendale Valley, a few miles north of Bury. My job was to hump around huge 14- and 16- foot flats, which were canvas boards depicting scenes from South Pacific, Carousel and Gilbert and Sullivan operettas, etc., and load them onto a wagon. We delivered these to various amateur dramatic societies around the region. I also managed to rent a bedsit on Walmersley Road in Bury and I hadn't been there very long when I made contact with Susan again and we began seeing each other for a while. There was an open coal fire in my bedsit and I made the place very cosy. I also began painting again, but only as a hobby, not in any professional capacity. I can remember one particular romantic, idyllic, evening when I sat drawing and painting Susan. Her lovely face was framed by the flickering firelight which set the room aglow, but I don't think my work really captured her loveliness. In fact, it was a lousy painting, one of my worst.

My job at Haslingden was poorly paid and travelling to and fro on the bus every day was working out to be rather a costly affair, which meant that I had very little money left, especially after I had been on the booze all weekend. Thus there were times when I was forced to go to work with no food in my belly and nothing to eat all day. This, as one can imagine, eventually began to take its toll on my health. But at least I was enjoying the work, as it was much more interesting than the other jobs I had done, and there was plenty of variety each day. I could also study Tony, the scenic artist, and pick up tips for my own painting. The problem was that I just couldn't afford to keep travelling all the way to Haslingden. Jobs were plentiful in those days and it was not uncommon for folk to be able to walk out of one job at lunchtime and straight into another the next day. I actually did this once. I was working on a building site and was late one morning, so the foreman shouted over, 'Do you know what f****** time we start?'

'No,' I replied, 'You always seem to be at it when I get here.' He sacked me on the spot, so I walked off the job with a two-fingered wave. I then crossed town to another building site and asked if they needed any labourers.

'Start tomorrow, eight o'clock.' It was as simple as that in those days.

I was employed in a large variety of occupations at one time or another. I worked in a scrap metal yard, had various mill jobs connected to the once-thriving cotton industry, on which Bury and other industrial towns and cities were built, and I was a forklift truck driver for a time. I even tried my hand as a grave-digger at Bury Cemetery. On my first day the foreman warned me that, 'It's heavy work, lad, so we'll start you on a little 'n'.' This meant that I was to dig a grave for a child, perhaps even a baby. This was heart-rending, but I recommend grave-digging to anyone who wants to know what it is like to be humbled. I soon transferred from grave-digging, nevertheless, to gardening, and I tried to put my absolute all into the work, but in the end what I was doing was mostly cutting grass and weeding. There was nothing creative about the job, so I was soon getting frustrated again.

After a while I was moved to a new base at Peel mills, where Sir Robert Peel had once owned buildings connected to the cotton trade, as well as bleaching works. My job was to mow the grass verges of the bypass and other areas nearby. Two of us were employed to do this job and we were mostly left to our own devices, with the foreman driving round in a van whenever he felt like it, which wasn't very often. The only trouble with this system was that I never knew when I would be caught out sitting down smoking, instead of working. The feller I worked with was called Alan Armstead. Alan burnt buckets of nervous energy just trying not to work.

I remember one particular morning when we had gone to open the lock-up in order to get out our mowers in readiness of starting work. 'Whoa!' said Alan, pointing to a small dark cloud drifting across the far distance of an otherwise blue sky. 'That'll be over us anytime soon, Steve,' he said. 'It isn't worth getting the mowers out,' he continued, as though heavy downpours were imminent. He never stopped hoping we would be rained off so that we could spend the day sitting in the cabin drinking tea, smoking and reading the newspapers, even on the most glorious of days. And then, if we were late getting the mowers out of the lock-up, Alan would say, 'Oh well, it's not worth bothering. It'll be brew time any minute. We'll get 'em out after.' So we would go and have a cup of tea, and just as we were about to get the mowers out Alan would find another reason for leaving them till later. Inevitably he would then say, 'It's not worth bothering now, it'll be lunchtime soon.' This once led to us going for a full eight-hour shift without ever getting the mowers out of the lock-up, which was no mean feat.

One day Alan failed to turn up for work and it began raining early in the morning, so I sat in the cabin drinking tea alone, which in some ways I was glad of, for this gave me an opportunity to read a new letter from Mum, which then started me thinking back to my childhood. Mum was learning to swim at the same time as Clive and I, when I was about 6 or 7 years of age. We were standing on the side of the pool when a kid came running past and pushed Clive into the water. None of us could swim as yet and so I looked up at Mum, wondering what to do. But she wasn't there, she was in the pool already and was trying to save Clive, despite the fact that she was both lame and unable to swim. Fortunately it had happened at quite a shallow place, so Mum and Clive were alright in the end. Mum was a brave woman in many different ways.

In her letter she explained how she had been training to be a guide at Burghley House, taking tourists round and showing them paintings, murals and artefacts that had been collected across the centuries, which seemed to be a perfect job for her. I thought back to when she used to take us to Bury Art Gallery, showing us the different paintings and other artworks. She particularly liked a painting titled *The Random Shot* by Landseer, which was of a female deer lying dead in the snow with its youngster looking on. My musings could not go on indefinitely, however, as the rain had now stopped and I had to get some work done.

Part of my job was to drive wooden stakes into the ground and bind them to rows of young trees or saplings, protecting them from the strong winds which often blew from the high Pennine moors surrounding the town of Bury, which huddles in the lower ground at the northern edge of the great plain of Manchester. Alan and I would set off with our wheelbarrows full of stakes and a metal detector, which we had bought in order to try to find Roman coins reputedly buried in the area. Thus we spent half our time driving stakes into the ground and binding trees and the other half sweeping that same ground, hoping to find buried treasure that would make us super-rich. In fact, metal detecting was about the only time Alan did any work at all.

As the weeks passed we ended up with a fine collection of rusty nails which weren't even from the Roman era, or any other historical era come to that, and not even a single coin – not even a modern-day penny. So in the end we gave up and sold the metal detector to a second-hand shop. The money we got for the thing was then spent at the pub, of course. I must say that I did enjoy this job to some extent, but again it was poorly paid and on such wages I couldn't possibly have saved for a house, or to get married, but more especially because I was spending half of my wage on booze.

I changed jobs often in an effort to get some relief from the tedium of my life. I don't know how I got there, but eventually I found myself in a job at the skin-yard, which was the worst of the worst – the absolute pits of a job. I would spend eight hours a day cutting ears from rancid skins, so that they could be used to fashion sheepskin coats. The atmosphere was heavy, in fact it stank to high heaven in that awful place, but what was most worrying, were the signs all around warning of the dangers of contracting anthrax. How on earth I ended up there I do not know, though very likely it was because that was all I could get at the time. I had started and finished so many jobs that there was probably nothing else left to apply for.

George was another mate from the youth club. He had grown up on what was known as the Springs Estate, which at the time was generally regarded as the roughest estate in town. George did so well in his exams that he qualified to attend Bury Grammar School. He was very good-looking and clever, but his family were very poor and didn't have the money to send him there, so he too had ended up leaving school at 15 and working in yet another of the cotton mills. As a young lad he was the scruffiest kid in class, but in later years was, and still is, always immaculately dressed. He and Hardy decided they would head for Torquay, the English Riviera, where they were intent on finding jobs, drinking beer and chasing girls.

One day I was cutting the ears from the stinking sheepskins with my knife when the foreman passed by, making comments regarding the speed at which I was working, and, as this continued, I had a terrible urge to stab him. 'Time to leave,' I told myself. I decided I would join Hardy and George in Torquay and I would hitch all the way in order to save money. Even though I would miss Susan, I couldn't take any more of the skin-yard and other job options had dried up.

The first lift I got was in a huge articulated lorry and the driver and I chatted well. He told me he could take me to London, which was more than half of my journey. During our chat he got on to the subject of brass bands and told me he played in one. I told him I had tried to learn the trumpet, among other instruments, but had failed miserably. I then told him I had been given lessons by Harold Moss, my granddad, and he was most impressed, as Harold Moss was, as I said, a leading figure in the world of brass bands. Our conversation eventually dried up and so we fell silent, staring out of the window at the passing fields and farms. I, for some reason, thought about the time I stayed with Royce Ainsley and his beautiful wife, Margaret, who was like a young Elizabeth Taylor.

I cannot remember a great deal of that part of my life, but it was when I was drawing the National Assistance Board's (NAB) money, so I was obviously out of work just then. All the NAB money would provide was a few quid to Royce for my keep, steak pudding, chips and peas at Colson's Café and that was about it – no money again for a week. I don't know what made me think of Royce and Margaret, but I will always be grateful for their kindness. They put a roof over my head when I had nowhere else to live. My thoughts then began straying back to myself and I started to wonder if maybe I was mentally ill, as I felt that my life up to that point had been so bizarre that it wouldn't be considered 'normal' by most people's standards. The term 'bipolar' had not been created then, so I diagnosed myself as manic-depressive. When I began writing this book I decided to leave out the depressing parts of my life as much as possible, as this would undoubtedly depress both myself and the reader. I was 21 by the time I hitched that lift and still I had no idea what my life was about. I did not know my destiny, but I did know my immediate destination: sunny Torquay.

After the lorry driver dropped me off just outside London, I tried desperately to get more lifts, to try to reach Torquay before nightfall, but sadly it just didn't happen, so I climbed up the banking and slept by the roadside. Whilst in dreamland,

I heard a strange noise nearby and when I plucked up enough courage to look to see what it was, I saw a small white pony that seemed to be curious as to who I was. Leaning over the fence, I stroked his head and then hugged him. He nuzzled his way closer to me – a lonely young man and a lonely young pony, supporting each other through the night. After this I got my head down on my bag, my coat over my shoulders and the pony wandered off, leaving me to enjoy a peaceful night's sleep. I dreamed of swimming naked with Susan in a vat of ale. As soon as it was light I was on my feet again and hitching along the road with my thumb up, as was the custom. I managed to get four more lifts before at last reaching Torquay; one was a very cold lift on the back of an open wagon.

I soon tracked down the address where Hardy and George were staying and we greeted one another with big hugs before getting our heads down. I slept on their floor. They had both found jobs on a building site, but I decided I would look for a job using the skills I had picked up at Buckley Hall. I got a job as kitchen porter in a hotel right on the seafront.

It was the beginning of the season and there were only about three of four guests in the hotel, so the chef would make breakfast and I would wash the pans. Then it was down to the beach. I got back for lunch and more pan washing, then away to the beach again. Same again for the evening meal, and that, basically, was my working day. I was getting three four-star meals and was able to sunbathe every single day – what a great job!

The early part of the season was idyllic, in fact, but as the summer wore on the crowds increased and the hotel filled up, so my job became extremely hard work. I had mountains of pans to scrub out three times a day and I also assisted in food preparation. It was hard graft, but at least I was learning useful tricks of the trade, such as how to fry eggs perfectly. I also learnt how to make hard-boiled eggs without them turning green and that as soon as a hot pan is finished with you put cold water in it immediately and this releases much of the stuck-on bits of food. I still do this today when I am cooking. I was learning positive skills, but sadly there were also some negative lessons, such as the drinking of scrumpy, which is a very strong cider principally brewed in the south-west of England.

This West Country cider was so strong that some pubs would only serve each customer half a pint at a time. We were enjoying a fun-filled summer on the south coast and so it wasn't long before Kevan Jackson, nickname Jacko, joined us down there. He had suffered a broken heart after his girlfriend dumped him and so he felt he needed to leave town, and we all ended up living together at Norrie's Rooming House. We rented two rooms, with three beds in one, and one bed in the other, which George slept in. It was very basic to say the least, the upside being that it was cheap. It turned into a baking-hot summer that year and I managed to get a deep tan for the first time in my life. My days were spent working hard, drinking hard and laughing. Such days were lightened even further when Hardy began performing his new and crazy routines for the benefit of the holidaymakers.

One late night after the pubs had closed we came across two guys kicking a football around and we joined in; others joined in too till we had two large teams playing against each other in the street. One team took off their shirts in order to be identified, and the other team kept theirs on. The game grew madder and madder until Jacko decided he would take off not only his shirt but everything else as well. One lad, a Liverpudlian, shouted, 'The guy in the nude, which side is he on?' Someone attempted a 35-yard drive in order to equalise, but he sliced his shot and the ball went straight through a window instead. That, of course, signalled the end of the game. Kev scrambled to pick up all of his clothes and we ran for it. Fortunately I didn't get the blame for that window, or I would probably have ended up back inside!

Most nights out finished up at The Yacht, which was a trendy venue where many young people gathered to see and be seen. Torquay had, and probably still does have, a language school and this attracted dozens of rich, beautiful blondes from Sweden, Denmark and Finland. None of us managed to chat any of them up though. Perhaps shouting, 'Hey-up, blondie!' from our second-floor window wasn't really sophisticated enough for these girls.

We occasionally procured dope and smoked it while discussing the possibilities of travelling the world, but at that time the term 'hippy trail' hadn't been coined. All four of us were trying to figure out what to do with the rest of our lives. Hardy was a skilled tradesman who could earn decent money in any town or city. Jacko and George were labouring on a building site, which didn't seem to hold much promise for the future, and I was still washing pans in that hotel kitchen.

I had gained a promotion though, as I was now the appointed breakfast chef, but without any increase in wages. This made me wonder if maybe I should train to be a proper chef. Part of me just wanted desperately to go out into the big wide world and make my fortune; then I could return to Bury and marry the lovely Susan – if she would have me, that is! However, my wages were so poor that I could hardly afford my train fare back to Bury, let alone have enough money for getting married and buying a house.

One of Hardy's new 'amusements' was to drop his trousers and stand semi-naked, chatting to girls, which caused quite a commotion in some pubs, as you can imagine. This was long before streaking and mooning had become the fashion, and the 'let it all hang out' hippy culture was still a long way off. One evening, after the scrumpy had taken its ruthless toll on my faculties, I went on a long run down to the sea front, where I jumped as high into the air as I could, before landing fully clothed in the sea and, with the waves crashing around me,

I struggled to get out. In fact it was quite a close call. I then dripped my way through the remainder of the evening in various pubs, which, no doubt, caused more than a little wonderment and amusement among the revellers.

It was while I was in Torquay, after having watched a film with the lads, and wondering about those actors on screen, that a germ of an idea took root and began forming. I had always been a bit of a class clown and was quite good at imitating people, so I began wondering how on earth those actors started in that business. I felt that if I could find out, then maybe that would be something I might try and do.

Whilst wandering home from the pub alone one evening, George picked up a rabbit out of someone's garden and brought it home as a present for the rest of us. It slept in a drawer that night, but was duly returned to its rightful owner the very next morning after a long search for the house, as George wasn't exactly certain where it was located. I am glad to be able to write that the rabbit was no worse for its unusual experience of lodging in a drawer for the night among strangers and strange surroundings.

George, Hardy and I, along with a friend called Dave Wood, who was a chef at Transparent Works Canteen, had spent some time living together at a rented house in Shepherd Street, Bury. Some of my fondest memories of that short spell in my life were of us all talking about our futures while drinking together, or listening to a radio show called *I'm Sorry, I'll Read That Again*, which was a precursor to the forming of Monty Python. It occurred to me while in Torquay that a lot of the conversations we were now having were almost exactly the same as those we had enjoyed at that rented house back in Bury. Two years on and our lives had not changed.

The son of the owner of the hotel where I worked was obviously a product of a public school, as he had a very refined accent and his manner was always 'upper class'. He would have been about 30 at the time, and whenever his father wasn't around he would torment me with patronising comments. One day when I was busy working in the kitchen he shouted for me to come and fetch some tins from the pantry, which was a cool room where foodstuffs were stored. I went into the pantry and there he began throwing tins at me, so fast that I couldn't keep up as I tried to catch them. I had a very strong compulsion to throw the tins right back at his smug face, but instead I just turned around, walked out of the kitchen and never went back, not even for my half day's pay that was owed. Buckley Hall had taught me much about discipline and self-control and it took a lot of inner strength for me to walk away, rather than drop the guy to the canvas.

I soon got a very similar job in another kitchen and on the second day I was scrubbing pans after the evening meal when I saw George and Hardy through the window, walking towards the kitchen door with sad expressions. My heart sank. Had something happened to Jacko? They handed me a piece of paper, it was a telegram and read 'Dad died today *stop* Love Mum *stop*'. My heart and mind jolted in unison. This man I called Dad – this man who I loved, this man who had looked after me all my childhood, this man that I hardly knew – had gone forever. Now I would never be able to stand and have a pint with him, and thank him for giving me food, shelter and protection. Now I could never find out why he had shown me such little attention. My emotions were in ribbons.

I told the chef what had happened and I went back to the house. I asked George if I could sleep in the single room that night, as I needed to let my mind take this in. I cried myself to sleep and felt guilty in the morning for not staying awake after hearing this terrible news. Hardy lent me some money to get to Stamford to be with Mum. I will keep this short, save to say that Mum had her much loved job and some very good friends who would be there for her.

Dad had had a long-standing heart condition and his heart had finally given up the struggle. I was so sad that he never managed to finally retire and take more time to enjoy his hobbies and his snooker. A death in any family brings with it such conflicting feelings that I cannot find suitable words. Tears are sometimes the only expression available. When the bleakness subsided I got myself back to Torquay and carried on. After all, what else was there to do?

The season was drawing to a close and so Hardy, George and Jacko would soon be heading back to Bury, but I had nowhere to go back to. Jacko was going to live with his parents. George was to live with his sister, Mary, and Hardy would return to live with his mother. Hardy invited me to stay with him and his mum till I sorted myself out, which offer I was grateful for, though I was as yet undecided as to what lay in the immediate future for me.

One afternoon, between lunchtime pan-scrubbing and evening meal pan-scrubbing, I escaped from the bad weather by going to the library, where I browsed through books and newspapers, as if I was searching for something; what, I didn't know, but then I noticed a newspaper titled *The Stage and TV Weekly*. I opened it from the back, as left-handers often do, and it jumped out at me: an advertisement reading, 'Mountview Theatre School, London. Two Year, Evenings and Weekends – Acting Course.' So that is how people become actors: they study! Now I had an answer. At the time I viewed this as a sign from heaven and after work I rushed home to tell Hardy, Jacko and George about these acting classes. I even put forward the idea that, as the holiday season was just about finished, why didn't all four of us make our way to London and try to become actors. The response to this suggestion was one mainly of mirth, followed by apathy and general mickey-taking. At that time, the idea of lads like us becoming actors was as distant a dream as us becoming astronauts, which made me realise that if I was going to do this, then I would have to do it alone. And so, alas, we parted with lots of hugging and tears held back as we said our manly goodbyes, after what had been a funny and glorious summer spent forging strong bonds that would last a lifetime.

In the years that followed, George got married and became the manager of a caravan site in Newquay. Jacko, or Kev, went back to a life as a semi-professional musician: writing songs and playing drums for Mobius Loop. And though we had all talked about world travel, having dreamed of it for so long, only one of us actually achieved it – 'Mad' Hardy.

Clive, my brother, was serving with the navy on HMS *Albion*, which was the main ship in the naval task force bound for the Indonesian Confrontation. This meant he would be separated from his new wife, Marie, for an indeterminate period, so she had gone to stay with my mum. I needed to get some money together if I was to get to London and train as an actor, so I decided that I would head for Stamford, where I was looking forward to seeing Mum again. She had now bought a little house in the town, as the rent-free bungalow on the estate had only been a perk of Dad's job. I went straight to Marie's place of work, the Central Wool Growers, and got a job easily.

During the sheep-shearing season all the farmers in the surrounding area would send their fleeces to the Central Wool Growers, where men, myself included, were hired to pile them almost to the roof of the building and, when required by the graders, to drag them over on 'bogeys' for inspection. It was hard and heavy work and we used baling hooks for lugging the wrapped fleeces around the place. Once the graders had shouted a particular name and farm, we would have to climb the piles and root out the right fleeces. It was heavy work and could be dangerous too.

Just how dangerous was brought home to us all one day when a young student who was temporarily employed there came crashing to the ground with a sickening thud and was buried under a big pile of fleece sacks. We managed to pull him out after some heavy work and he was taken to hospital with a fractured collarbone and concussion. Personally, I don't think that danger can be prevented in life, as the whole life's journey is one of danger and of risk. All we can do is try to minimise those dangers as best we can.

The job attracted some real oddballs and misfits, and I soon realised that studying some of these characters would stand me in good stead if I could begin training as an actor. Though I didn't quite feel that I had discovered my real destiny, I certainly felt that I was on the road to it. Some days I would ring in sick and go for a walk by the river, or go to the library, where I began reading Stanislavski's *Creating a Role*. I also read about the famous Actors Studio in New York, where Marlon Brando, Rod Steiger, James Dean and other legends had all studied.

After the graders had finished their job the fleeces were all tightly baled and I was given the job of driving them to a storage building across town. They were transported on a small flatbed wagon and the bales needed to be secured before setting off for the stores, so I learnt how to rope and sheet these properly. After a few weeks of doing this job one of the bosses wandered by and shouted, 'You look like a real wool man now, Steve.' I reflected on this comment and thought to myself, I'm not a real wool man! I am simply playing the part. It was then that it dawned on me that nothing of my working life seemed real.

It was becoming clearer and clearer that the jobs I had been employed to carry out over the first few years of my working life were simply jobs that I had been forced into because of circumstances and that none of these involved my soul. I was simply acting the part. I had imitated the other wool men and learnt the job by doing so, but the difference between them and me was that my heart just wasn't in it, or in any of the jobs I had been forced into in order to make a living. Although, with jobs like that maybe nobody has their hearts involved. What I didn't realise at the time, though, was that I was actually learning whilst doing these jobs. I was learning skills that might prove useful when playing working-class characters. My mind wandered back to the gypsies, tinkers and scrap metal dealers I had studied in Colson's Café in Bury, and I hoped that one day, if I could find a way to become an actor, I would get the chance to play characters just like them.

One evening after work I was sitting chatting to Mum and she reminded me of the time when I was about 8 and some kid threw a stone and hit me in the eye. The injury was quite serious and there was a possibility that I would lose the eye. She then told me that Dad had said to her at the time that if I did lose it, I could have one of his as a replacement. Fortunately I didn't lose it, but as she was telling me this, tears streamed down my cheeks. The man I called Dad, who had shown me so little affection, who had struggled to even pay me any attention, must obviously have had love for me in his heart. Mum then told me that Dad had grown up in a household where the atmosphere was cold and hard and unloving. Being affectionate was not considered manly in the world he'd known as a boy. Mum also said that Dad could be loving and affectionate with her, but that he found it very difficult with anyone else.

5

A Different Test

I hold to the doctrine that with ordinary talent and extraordinary perseverance, all things are attainable.
Thomas Buxton

Working in the wool industry had enabled me to save some money, but not much. Yet I felt it was time to head for London. I sensed that Mum thought this was yet another of my hair-brained schemes and she reminded me of my last struggle to survive in the Capital. Nevertheless, she wished me well and gave me fifty quid, saying that Dad would have wanted me to have it. He hadn't left anything for Clive and I in his will; everything went to Mum, which didn't really amount to much. My job hadn't paid very well, so this money from Mum was very welcome indeed. I gave her a hug and set off.

I had done plenty of hitch-hiking over the years, but I felt that those days were over, so I got on a train for London instead. The first thing I did on arriving was to go and register at a catering agency. They sent me to various pub restaurants and hotels where a kitchen porter was needed. This meant that I was able to eat for free, but, as yet, I still hadn't found anywhere to live. I may have gone up in the world from when I was a hitch-hiker, but I was still sleeping rough. Accommodation agencies didn't help much either, as they would send me on wild goose chases to bedsit addresses which didn't exist, or was it that I just couldn't find them? So I slept in Hyde Park with my little alarm clock by my side, dreaming of becoming an actor. It was summertime and I had lots of past experience of sleeping outdoors. I think I spent over a week sleeping rough and working at the Hong Kong and Shanghai Bank staff restaurant before I managed to rent a bed in a shared room at Camden Town; it was cheap and rough but was certainly a step-up or two from the park bench and the chilled night air.

In those days Camden wasn't the up-market area it is today and I would share a room with passing lorry drivers or Irish navvies who were working in London on a temporary basis. On my first night there, during a conversation with one of these lorry drivers, we agreed that the world would be a better place if wealth was shared. I fell fast asleep and when I awoke the next morning he had gone, along with my transistor radio. The next evening I went to find Mountview Theatre School.

I applied for an audition and I had about a week to wait before I faced my big challenge. I was doing my best to be very careful with my money, as, if I was accepted, I didn't know just how much I would need for tuition fees. But when I finished work I would call into the nearest pub and have a pint while learning 'To be or not to be' from Shakespeare's *Hamlet* and a speech from Edward Albee's *The Zoo Story*.

We never studied Shakespeare at school, so I was finding it difficult to understand the language of his day. In that speech there is a line which reads, 'To sleep no more.' Hamlet is contemplating suicide and if he were to die he would sleep no more.

This led me to think that he would be in a permanent sleep if he did kill himself – so what did he mean by this? And then it dawned on me, or at least I thought I knew what Shakespeare was getting at. I believe he was saying that to die is no more than a sleep, which is nothing to be afraid of. To sleep no more! The speech now began making sense, as it goes on to read, 'But that the dread of something after death, that undiscovered country, from whose bourn, no traveller returns, puzzles the will.' We tend to fear death because we do not know what comes after it and this is what this speech is all about. If we knew that death was just like a dreamless sleep, I don't think we would fear it at all, but 'life' can often be frightening.

The day of my audition arrived and I knew that this was make or break time – or at least that is how it felt at the time. As I sat waiting to go into the room a sense of destiny seemed to fill my soul. The door suddenly opened, making me jump. 'Steve Halliwell!' In a trance I went inside. Three total strangers stared at me. This is it! This is it! Here we go! I was so hopelessly nervous while delivering my speech that I felt as though I had an out-of-body experience. For a fraction of a second it seemed as if I was watching myself reciting Shakespeare's words. After it was all over I had to hang around and wait while other potential students were being seen.

Peter Coxhead, the principal and founder of Mountview Theatre School, eventually came out of the audition room and approached me. Had I been accepted? I could hardly breathe as I awaited the school's decision, yet part of me didn't want to hear what he had to say, just in case I had failed to get in. I needn't have worried, however, as he gave me the news that I had, indeed, got in. I was so happy and grateful and in my head I kept saying 'thank you, thank you, thank you' without really knowing to whom I was addressing those words – to Peter Coxhead, to God, to the universe? I didn't know, but boy was I excited. That is when, more than ever before, I had a feeling that told me this was indeed what I was meant to do; that my bizarre life so far had been leading to this moment of triumph. And though this may have been a small triumph in the general scheme of things, it was certainly a huge triumph, a triumph on a grand scale in fact, to me. I headed for the pub that evening and celebrated, but, owing to my weakness for the drink and the euphoric mood which enveloped me, I almost spent the week's money on whisky.

The following day my former euphoria subsided somewhat when I began wondering if everyone was accepted in order that the school could get their hands on those tuition fees, just like that loopy school I'd been sent to as a boy. That, of course, is the way moods rapidly swing with manic-depressive people. You can be as high as a kite one day, and then suicidal the next. Another depressing thought was that I had been told I had to buy some black ballet tights for the movement classes. That evening I resolved that I would do whatever I had to do in order to become an actor. Back at the lodgings, I continued sharing a room with complete strangers and always tried to engage them in conversation before going to sleep. I so wanted to tell someone that I was about to begin a two-year acting course, but didn't feel that these lads would have any interest in such things.

There had been a recent breakthrough in the acting profession when working-class people such as Michael Caine, Albert Finney and Tom Courtney had found much success. This boosted my confidence that a working-class lad like myself would have a chance of making it, but as early as my first class, which was movement, I realised that everyone else in the room was middle-class. I tried to talk in a neutral accent, as I was quite a good mimic and thought I could pull this off – I didn't want the other students to know that I was a working-class lad from Lancashire. I decided to try this new accent on one of the girls and she simply replied, 'Hey-up lad, where are you from then?' She had mimicked my accent. So I had obviously done a poor job of attempting to hide who I really was.

During the first movement class the teacher instructed us to write down the correct way to walk. I had written down, 'Heel, ball, toe,' about seventeen times before thinking how ridiculous this was. Then we all had to get up and walk across the room and study how each of us walked. I had never before been particularly conscious of how I walked, but, when it was my turn, nerves made me walk in a peculiar way, which resulted in quite a bit of laughter. Fortunately, other students were nervous too and this led to more odd and amusing walks that evening.

Along with the movement classes we also did voice, improvisation and even fencing classes, which was all preparation for a career on the stage. We had to learn speeches and analyse scripts, as well as having a long list of books to read. There were also end-of-term productions, which were performed in the little adjoining theatre. Mountview was then only conducting part-time classes and had not yet developed into the prestigious full-time acting school that it is today. The little theatre was often hired by professional companies for the production of their plays. Apart from pantomime and the one play Mum had taken me to see when I was only a small boy, I hadn't seen any other live theatre at all. The play Mum took me to see was fascinating, but I was far too young to have known what it was all about.

Now I was involved with acting I tried to get to see every production that was staged in the little theatre. Part of my reading included Stanislavski's *An Actor Prepares*, Grotowski's *Towards a Poor Theatre*, Shakespeare, Pinter, Beckett – in fact, anything that I felt would enhance my skills as an actor. I also continued to study characters in the local pubs, only more avidly than I had before, now that I knew there was real purpose in this.

I also listened attentively to various London accents and tried to distinguish north London from south London, or east London from west. I believe I didn't achieve much in this regard, but still I tried and tried, also adding to my repertoire by practicing American accents. I had already done an American accent, during my audition speech for Edward Albee's *The Zoo Story*, which resulted in my acceptance into the school, so maybe I had pulled it off. The more I got to meet and talk to second-year students, the more I realised that there were indeed other working-class lads in attendance; they just had southern accents, that's all. I was beginning to distinguish between southern middle-class and working-class accents, which surely meant I was making progress.

After I had been attending the school for a while, some American students arrived, which gave me a first-hand opportunity to listen to their varying accents. One of the teachers, Terry Meech, I found to be very sympathetic and understanding of my need to work incredibly hard if I was going to eradicate my northern accent, which I felt I needed to do. In teaching drama it is generally thought that a standard English accent, or RP (received pronunciation), is preferable, for one could assume a variety of accents for particular roles, or at least that was the case at the time. Lots of stereotyping was going on then, and I am sure it still is today, in some cases at least, but a northern regional accent was then equated with unintelligence, and a southern middle-class accent being considered the opposite. This meant that if I was to be taken seriously as an actor, I would have to change the way I spoke. Whether I agreed with this or not was irrelevant, because, as I stated earlier, whatever I had to do to be an actor was fine by me.

The first end-of-term production I was involved with was *The Balcony* by Genet, which was a play set in a brothel, with quite a complex political comment running through it. I cannot say that I fully understood it then, and I'm not sure I do now, but the play really gave me a chance to use some of the skills I was learning. I played a couple of small parts in the play, one, ironically, being that of a beggar!

I became more and more manic about being an actor and my social skills suffered as a result, meaning that I spent much of my time alone. I also hated sharing a room with complete strangers. So I decided I would move out of my rented room, well, sort of. The front door of the house was left unlocked all night and there was a large armchair in the shared bathroom. This meant that I could sneak back late at night and sleep in the big chair, after locking the bathroom door of course. This saved lots of rent money until I eventually found somewhere else to live.

I rented a room in a house at Wood Green that was owned by a Greek woman who fought like cat and dog with her daughter. I sometimes wondered if I should call the police, the fighting was that fierce, but then two minutes later I would hear the both of them laughing and joking as if nothing had happened. They kindly gave me a job in their rag trade business and I would work with the Greek women, picking cotton from dresses and loading and unloading vans. They played a particular Greek song over and over again on their little record player until I knew it by heart. I had no idea what I was singing about, but my mimicking skills allowed me to parrot the words of the singer, which were, of course, Greek. This made the women laugh a lot and I think they grew quite fond of me. The daughter would sometimes cook me a meal, which was always fish and red beans, while her mother would ask, 'Do you like my daughter, Stavros, hey? She look English, yeah?' And yes, I did like her, but I was determined to let nothing distract me from becoming an actor.

The very first time I went into the little theatre bar at Mountview, I sat down as two young men walked in. The bar was crowded and one of the young men said to the other, 'Oh, we're going to have to stand at the bar with the men.' The other young man responded, 'Men? There's not a man in here!' I had never before seen camp, gay people and I must say that at the time it came as quite a shock. The term 'coming out of the closet' was not yet in common usage, but those two were obviously very comfortably out of it!

The next play I was involved with was *The Hostage* by Brendan Behan. I cannot remember a great deal about it, but I do remember playing a few small parts in the production. The important thing was that I was getting opportunities to go on stage and act in front of a live audience, and until you have done that you really do not know whether or not you have what it takes to be an actor.

I did some work about this time for an odd job/cleaning agency and landed on my feet when I was sent to clean the guttering of a large house which belonged to a Jewish couple. Helen Silverman was the lady of the manor and she showed deep concern when I told her I was studying to be an actor. She said to me, 'You could starve three times a day trying to be an actor,' and promptly made me a sandwich. Rye bread, stuffed with salt beef and pickled gherkin, accompanied by wholegrain mustard. At the time, I had never tasted such good food. Her husband was a lawyer and they were obviously very wealthy. Mrs Silverman was a wonderful lady who looked after me whenever I did any work at her house, plying me with all kinds of different delicacies, which she hoped would keep my starvation at bay.

The school was offered an opportunity to perform two plays on the American stage during a student festival over there, so, in order to raise much-needed funds for this project, we all decided to take part in a sponsored walk from Cambridge to London, approximately 50 miles. We walked through the night and I joined in, even though I knew I could not afford to go to America. I wanted to know if I could complete such a long walk – I did. I was one of only four students to finish and I hadn't trained beforehand. I even walked in my normal shoes, as training shoes had not yet become widely available in the UK and I had no boots.

The principal of the school offered me the part of Benvolio in *Romeo and Juliet*, but rather than accept, which is what I so wanted to do, I had to inform him that my job was so poorly paid that I would not be able to go with them to America. Thus, he gave the part to someone else. However, one positive thought I got from being offered the part was that Peter, the principal, must have seen something in me during what was, after all, still my first year at the school.

I do not know just how many miles it was, but I often had no money to get the bus from Wood Green to Crouch End, so I would regularly walk to and from class. I was determined that whatever obstacles came my way, I would simply climb over them, go around them, go right through them: do anything to prevent failure at what had become my real passion in life. Nothing was going to stop me from becoming an actor and my resolve was strengthened when I thought about the hard life my grandfather had lived, digging coal for a living whilst working a mile or so underground. In fact, an oft-told story in our family was how my grandfather, Harold Moss, when a young man, would finish his shift at the mine and then, on returning home, would go upstairs and practice his trombone. There his family would find him, still covered in coal dust and clutching his trombone to his chest after having fallen fast asleep. He was made of sterner stuff than I was, but, still, determination made me push myself beyond limits which inevitably came my way.

At the end of the first year we were asked if there was anything we would like to try – anything that we hadn't done in class. I heard myself reply, 'Yes, I'd like to try going in front of the class to see if I can make you all laugh.' So, up I got, without any clue as to what I was going to do in order to accomplish this. There was a table and chair in the room, so I sat at the chair and imagined I was in a room all alone and bored out of my mind. I would pretend to hear noises at the door and then pretend to peer through a window, hoping for something to happen; just a man alone in a room, bored. I gradually built-up the scene until I was peering under the table as if someone was there. It is very hard to describe exactly what I was doing, but it worked, as my performance got everyone laughing. All I can say is that I created a character best described as a forerunner to Mr Bean. My creativity withered soon after, but I still got a round of applause from the other students, and from Peter Coxhead, which was very gratifying. After this improvisation and after I had performed an extract from *The Form*, by N.F. Simpson, I sensed a change in the attitude of the school staff towards me, as they were beginning to see that I did have something that was a little out of the ordinary.

Due to boredom and an insatiable desire for new experiences, I changed my job many times. I worked for Metal Box for a time, which meant standing on the end of yet another production line and piling tobacco tins into cardboard boxes. I worked for Smith's Crisps as a fork-lift truck driver, which was a job I had done before. This machine, however, was what they called a reach-truck, one on which the operator stood up and which had forks that came out sideways. It was a rickety old thing that I couldn't operate very well. In fact, after bursting several sacks of powdered potato and accidentally taking out the office window with the raised forks, I decided to leave. I had spent half a day causing a few hundred pounds worth of damage, and was gone. After that I worked for a small engineering firm, which meant drilling holes in brackets all day. I didn't really mind what I did, as long as I could try to keep boredom at bay and could continue with my classes during the evenings and weekends.

I cannot remember exactly how the deterioration began, but I do know that it came about as a result of the old and familiar problem of drinking too much.

There is a blur between working at the engineering firm and sleeping rough in an old car at a scrap-yard close to the school.

I was homeless and jobless and was just about scraping through on the dole but I would never miss a class. I had left what few belongings I possessed with a fellow student who rented a room above the school, so I would wash and change there. I cannot remember what excuse I came up with for leaving my suitcase there, as I didn't tell anyone I was sleeping rough, but one evening Peter Coxhead called me into his office and said that he needed to speak with me. He asked me quite a number of questions and then said that my appearance was becoming rather odd. My hair and beard had grown long again and I hadn't changed my clothes for days, possibly even weeks.

He could obviously see that I was in a poor mental state. He then told me that a job as caretaker at the school was soon going to become available, as well as a room for rent above the school. 'Are you interested?' he asked. Was I interested? He couldn't have known that what he told me that evening as good as saved my life and I bless him to this day for his kindness. From that time on almost my entire day was spent at the school. Whistling and singing to myself, I would sweep the theatre and continue on with my dream.

Opposite the room where I lodged was a classroom that had in it an old piano, so I spent quite a bit of my free time tinkering with the ivories. I was attempting to make the three chords I knew into a concerto, though I was endlessly thinking about acting. What style of acting would I develop? Would I be any good at it? These were just a couple of the questions I continually asked myself. Comedy seemed to be the more natural direction, but I also felt that I would like to have a go at serious acting too. I had a leaning towards roles which dealt with big issues regarding the human condition. My circumstances had improved and so I kept off the alcohol for a while, which was made easier by the fact that I had no money left over for drink. I would buy some cigarettes, some food, pay the rent and my tuition fees in instalments and, lo and behold, my money would be gone.

At the launderette one day, while watching my life tumbling over and over in the machine, it suddenly dawned on me that I was having virtually no contact with the opposite sex, so I vowed to resolve that matter. I quite fancied a student from Ghana who was attending the segregated black actors' course (sadly, they could get away with such things in those days). So, with the help of a few beers (I scraped enough money together by going without food), I chatted her up, letting her know in no uncertain terms that I fancied her. She responded positively and we began dating. I took her out to the cinema a couple of times, but not much happened between us. Then one day she came to my room and in a heated few moments it was brought home to me just how much I had been missing physical contact with the opposite sex.

Nothing much came of our relationship, but we did go out on a few more occasions, only to be glared at by both white and black people alike. It was rare to see a white boy and black girl together at the time (it sounds like the dark ages now, but was the norm then), but I consoled myself with believing that we were doing a positive thing in breaking down the racial mistrust which was so prevalent in society. For my part, I was very proud to have such a beautiful and sexy girl on my arm.

I enjoyed brief encounters with one or two other drama students, but no real relationship developed; maybe because my mental state was still a problem. The best way I can describe it is that I seemed to want to live a pretend life, not a real one. I was constantly studying people, continually making notes of how this gesture meant such a thing, or that mannerism indicated this or that – all things I could use to develop as an actor, but as regards living a real life, well, that was almost non-existent.

There was the 'in crowd' group of potential actors and actresses at the school, always engaged in non-stop chatter and gossip, but I could not find anyone who I could have a serious conversation with about the art of acting, if, indeed, acting is an art. Or is it a craft? Maybe acting is a craft which can be raised to the level of art? Such were the questions I wanted to discuss, but whenever I raised such subjects the conversation would only last for a few exchanges before veering back to the usual small talk and gossip. I felt as though I had little in common with the other students. I saw myself as a serious person who wanted to be a serious artist. Perhaps I was being pretentious and would have had more fun if I had just joined in the gossip.

The time was fast approaching for my final production at the school and, because of the comic skills I had developed and put on show, I was given my first lead role, as Khlestakov in Gogol's *The Government Inspector*. The full-time school had by now just started and, because there were only a few students, I was also asked to perform in a play for one of the new teachers. I felt a lot of responsibility and pressure, as I was to appear in two productions, playing the lead role in one of them. My nerves began getting bad, and then very bad. On the afternoon of my first reading of *The Government Inspector*, which would start that evening at seven-thirty, I sat going over and over the script. There was a gentle knock at my door; then it opened and a hand appeared with two of its fingers holding a tablet.

The hand belonged to Frank, an ex-Mountview student, and the tablet was LSD. I had asked Frank to try to get it for me so that I could find out what all the fuss was about, but that had been weeks before. Frank stood grinning, his long copper-coloured hair half hiding his seemingly demonic eyes. Part of me just wanted to run – run from the responsibility of a big lead role, and part of me wanted to run from Frank. I told him what I was doing that evening and he said the effects would have worn off by then. Wanting some relief from the pressure I was under, I weakened. Frank and I downed a tablet apiece. I had heard the expression 'bad trip' and very quickly I was having one. Time was soon just a word. I couldn't work out if I had just spoken or if it was Frank who had said something. Or was I thinking about speaking but hadn't said anything yet? Or was it Frank thinking of saying a few words? I couldn't go on to the rehearsal in this state and so got myself over to Frank's flat and hid away for, I think, hours. So yes, I missed that first rehearsal.

I lost the lead role before I had even begun rehearsing it. Peter Coxhead said that my attitude was totally unacceptable and unprofessional and that, if I wanted to pursue an acting career, I would have to change my thinking. I had totally let this man down – a man who had shown such faith in me, who had found me a job and a place to stay. I felt terrible. This also resulted in me being taken out of the full-time production altogether. Because of my manic-depressive personality and my inclination towards rebellion, I had landed back at what seemed to be square one.

After much soul-searching, I eventually picked myself up, dusted myself off and got on with playing a small character-part I had been offered in my final production. Things didn't work out too badly for me, as several of the other students admiringly said how it must have been hard for me after having lost the lead in the play. Thus the admiration of my peers made up in some small way for what I had lost, though I still wasn't proud of myself for having taken a self-destructive course once again.

A couple of weeks remained before my two-year course would finally be over and so I decided to write to Susan to ask her if she was with anyone and, if not, would she like to come down to London for a few days? To my delight, Susan responded and accepted my invitation. She arrived in London shortly after and it was lovely to see her again. I was worried about what I was going to do once the acting course ended and I even began wondering what life would be like if I returned to live in Bury. These thoughts, coupled with what had happened towards the end of my course due to my stupid behaviour, brought on the usual depression, but I did my utmost to keep this at bay so that I could have a bit of fun watching Susan enjoy the bright lights of London.

We grew much closer during her visit and Susan said that we could go and stay with her mum and dad after the course was finished, till we sorted something out. And that is exactly what we did. Susan was working in a cotton mill at the time and when we got back to Bury I signed on the dole, while writing lots of letters to theatre companies in search of work. Fortunately, and to my delight, I had a quick response from the Bolton Octagon Theatre, which is only a few miles from Bury. One of the actors was due to leave and they needed someone as an actor/assistant stage manager. I had told them all about my background in Lancashire and that I had grown up approximately 6 miles from Bolton. I had also told them all about my grandfather's history in brass bands, though I also told a lie, which I wasn't proud of. I had written in my letter that I had played Khlestakov in Gogol's *The Government Inspector*.

My audition and interview with the artistic director, Wilfred Harrison, went very well indeed and I was offered the first acting job I had applied for. My professional debut saw me playing seven different parts in a play called *The Sunday Walk*. I played, among others, Man in Black, Stranger, Man at Bar and half of The Passing Couple. I only had a few lines to learn for the whole piece, but it was an acting job, which enabled me to get my provisional Equity Card. From now on, instead of signing on the dole as a builder's labourer, I could sign on as an actor.

During a production of a musical version of Molière entitled *The Mock Doctor*, Wilfred Harrison, who was playing the lead, had to be pushed off the stage while standing on a two-wheeled cart. He was 6 feet 4 inches tall and well built, meaning he was very heavy, so I was to do the pushing. During one performance he stood a little too near the front of the cart and as a result it tipped slightly, making him wobble, but he managed to stop himself from falling and the performance went on without mishap till the interval. After the applause had died down Wilfred asked what had happened to the cart. I said that he had been standing too near to the front of it and that is why it had tipped, but he said to me, 'No, no, no. You were acting, weren't you? Don't act, just push the cart.' Don't act? I was certain that is what I had been employed to do – to act! Wilfred played all the lead roles himself and was very much of the old-school of actor–manager. Still, I couldn't complain too much, as I was learning my trade all the time, and I was being paid to do so.

As well as acting small parts, I was an assistant stage manager, which basically meant that I did a variety of jobs, including working on the sets, carrying out off-stage sound cues and going around begging, borrowing or stealing stage props. For instance, I would go to the nearby shops and ask if we could borrow a typewriter, which would be used on-stage and returned once the performance was finished. In return they would receive two free tickets and a free advert in the programme. Most shopkeepers would happily oblige. This I would do during the day, while also rehearsing for the next play, and then I would appear in the play during the evening. This meant long working hours with only Sundays off. After I had paid the tax man, I brought home about £13 a week. I had moved out of Susan's family home to be nearer the theatre, so I saw very little of her and, inevitably, this put a strain on our relationship.

I appeared in my very first pantomime at the Bolton Octagon Theatre. The production was *The Owl and the Pussycat* and I played a fish. The costume had an open fish mouth where my face appeared. To me this made it look like the fish had swallowed a man, which I felt was ludicrous. I appeared in several other productions at the Bolton theatre and enjoyed it tremendously, but already I could see that working such long hours would eventually destroy my relationship with Susan. I realised that I would soon have to choose between the job and her. Was I going to sacrifice my future with Susan in order to pursue my acting career? Or should I sacrifice my acting career in order to settle down, get married and start a family with Susan? I found myself in an unenviable position and finally settled this dilemma by giving up my job at the theatre.

I went back to live with Susan and her family and got a job at Courtaulds, in Bury. This company dyed man-made fibres and I stood at the end of a baling machine working one of three different shifts – seven till three, three till eleven or eleven till seven. When the alarm sounded, it would always take me a bit of time to figure out which shift I was on. At least I was getting far better pay than I had as an actor and this enabled Susan and I to begin saving for the wedding and for a deposit on a house.

Locally, there was a standard joke about Courtaulds: that their trade was producing skeletons. 'You will see them all walking up the road at seven in the morning,' it was said, meaning that it wasn't a particularly healthy environment in which to work. At the time, though, I felt that I had done the right thing, that I had made the right decision. It seemed to me, and I kept telling myself, that real people and real life were much more important than the pretend world of theatre.

6

A Flight of Fancy

Without work all life goes rotten. But when work is soul-less, life stifles and dies.

Albert Camus

I shared a bedroom at Susan's parents' home with her older brother, John. George, her younger brother, was away in the army. Henry and Marjorie, Susan's mum and dad, had to be respected, so Susan and I decided we would not sleep together at their house. However, this resolve was sorely tested and, once John had moved away after getting a job as an engineer, I did sneak into her bedroom on more than one occasion.

The shift-work was making me ill, so I decided I would try to get a job with more sociable hours. I went to work with Chris and Pete Snape, helping on their coal rounds.

I bagged up the coal, loaded the sacks onto a truck and then delivered them around town. At first we went out in pairs so that I could learn the routine; my first day on the job alone, I reversed over a rock at the side of a driveway and tipped about ten sacks of coal onto the ground. It took a long time for me to sort out the anthracite coal from the duck-egg coal and I was so late back the yard was locked. Not a great start. It was hard, heavy work and, with no leather back protection as yet, sometimes Susan had to point out that there was blood on my shirt.

As the wedding day approached, I began having some reservations, thinking that maybe my life in the future would not include the profession I had grown to love so much – acting. I was very much in love with Susan and wanted to be with her. Not being with her was out of the question, in fact, so I continued hoping that some day in the future I could once again try my hand at acting. The wedding day arrived and my bride looked beautiful. I was so proud to have her on my arm and to know that from now on she was going to be known as Mrs Halliwell. Henry and Marjorie let us have their double bed that evening, but Sue and I drank heavily during the celebrations that all we got up to was a deep, drunken sleep, the air full of alcohol fumes and the sound of snoring!

Bury Town Centre was due for demolishing and rebuilding and so there were plenty of labouring jobs available, which I applied for as I knew that I would never make a real coalman. I became a dumper-truck driver and general dogsbody around the building site. Although the pay was decent and I knew quite a number of the lads also working on the building site, I was still saddened to see those old streets and historic buildings flattened without ceremony. Princess Street was no more and its character-full pubs were forever gone, including the Queens Arms, where my brother had courted his wife, Marie, whose parents were the landlord and landlady.

I remember the King's Head, where Eric 'Wally' Wilson fought with three soldiers because they were chatting-up his then girlfriend, Joan Ainsley. The fight ended without a victor. The Queens Arms was frequented by Frank Dock,* who slept rough and was a raging alcoholic. He often slept at the brickyard, where the kilns provided some welcome warmth and so he was usually covered in red brick dust. I can remember Frank shouting in the street, 'Frankie Vaughn [a well-known entertainer at that time] got paid five hundred pounds for singing inside the Theatre Royal, and I got fined a fiver for singing outside!' This was just one of his many arrests for being drunk and disorderly.

The Coach and Horses was where Janet resided. She was a big husky-voiced landlady who would often say, 'Don't you knock my whisky over. I'd rather see blood spilt.' And blood was indeed often spilt there, as fights were common. One glorious bout was fought between Norman Crabtree and 'Jan the Pole'. The Three Crowns, another pub on Princess Street, was known locally as The Three Dollars. Another ale house around the corner was The Pineapple, nicknamed The Chunky.

A Boots store was being built in the new town centre and something had gone wrong with the planning. Where there should have been a large window, there was now a large wall. I was told to knock it down.

'How?' I asked.

'Get on your dumper-truck and drive into it,' was the reply. So with only a plastic helmet for protection, I drove straight into a 30-foot wall and it came crashing down all around me. I had to jump off the truck and run for my life.

Monty Python had started on television and I was an avid fan. It was while we were watching this programme one evening that Sue said she didn't feel very well and needed to go

---

* Note this name has been changed here and throughout to protect the individual's identity.

to the toilet. As she made her way upstairs she collapsed, the blood draining from her face. The ambulance came and rushed her to hospital. I sat waiting while the doctor examined her and I could hear him speaking on the phone to the blood bank, saying, 'This girl won't wait long – it has to be now.' So I knew that Susan was in serious trouble. A taxi with blood and a police escort sped from Manchester as the doctor told me that she had suffered an ectopic pregnancy – the foetus had started to grow in her fallopian tube – which had then caused internal bleeding. My prayers were no longer directed to the universe, or anywhere else, but directly to God, and Susan was saved, but sadly she lost an ovary.

Sue's dad owned a motorbike and he would let me borrow it to go and visit Susan during the evenings. She was a strong and fit girl and so recovered quite quickly. We hadn't even known she was pregnant, so we just had to accept that, for whatever reason, it wasn't to be.

Some of our friends, George and Christine among them, had all decided to go over to Jersey in order to find jobs for the summer season. Susan and I had saved quite a bit of money for a deposit on a house, but in the end, after much disagreement, we decided to join our friends in Jersey. The first couple of weeks were just like being on holiday. I hired a car and we toured the island, staying at cheap guesthouses until, finally, the money nearly ran out. Then, in desperation, we were forced to find jobs and somewhere to stay.

We were tipped off that it was best to go to where the local paper was printed and to get one hot off the press, run to a phone box and telephone the ads for vacant rooms. Susan and I did exactly that and found a small bedsit. Then we both found jobs very quickly. Sue worked in hotels as a silver service waitress and my first job there was as a laundry delivery man. I would haul huge baskets of clean laundry to hotels and pick up the equally huge baskets of dirty laundry. This was known as a 'job and finish'. I had many hotels to deliver to, and pick up from, during each day and the faster I could do it, the more time I had for enjoying the local beach scene. Although it was hard work, I must say that I did enjoy swimming and lolling around on the beach almost every day.

Jersey was full of rich people who were looked after by poor people, just like most other places around the world, I suppose, only on a smaller scale. Our days consisted of work, sunshine and drinking during the evenings. Hardy was also working in Jersey, on a land reclamation job, but he was living on the other side of the island, close to where he worked, so I didn't see a great deal of him.

A building job came available which was better paid than the laundry work. So my new boss was Charlie, a big bricklayer, originally from Bolton. I was employed to help a young millionaire extend his already large house. I was also to help dig a channel for a telephone cable so that he could have a telephone by his swimming pool. He owned several cars and an aeroplane. He told us he had made his money over in Ireland, and had become very wealthy before he had reached the age of 30. He didn't tell us, however, exactly how he had made his money.

I would sometimes accompany Charlie to a builders' yard that was owned by a friend of his. He was an Irishman who had been in Jersey since before the Second World War and he told us stories about the German invasion of the island. He owned quite a large piece of land and if he had sold it I am sure he could have retired a wealthy man, but instead he hung on to it. His land was full of building materials and some chickens. He told us that they were originally battery hens and that when he had first got them they had all stood in a row, not knowing they were able to move.

Even though I was fit, healthy and sun-tanned, and living life to the full on that beautiful island, I was still not content, as I had pangs to continue my career as an actor. Some actors become very wealthy, but most do not, so my desire to be an actor was nothing to do with wanting to be rich. My desire was more to do with my need for a creative outlet – the need to put my soul into something I loved doing. Not only could I not put my whole self into my work, but my heart wasn't in my leisure time either.

It was the era of the disco, which was not really my type of music. I wanted to be in a wine bar with candles burning in empty wine bottles, discussing literature, art, music and theatre. If there were any such places in Jersey, I never found one.

The season was soon over and with the onset of autumn it was time to fly back home. My first ever flight had been on coming to Jersey and I hadn't particularly enjoyed it, nor did I enjoy the return flight. Back in Bury, Sue continued working as a silver service waitress and I got a job in a builders' yard as a yard man, assisting the mechanics and doing all the odd jobs around the place. The nagging feeling that I had blown my chance of becoming a successful actor by leaving Bolton Octagon was beginning to plague me, so I said to Susan, 'I want to save up and go back to London, to see if I can make a career for myself as an actor.' Susan seemed happy in Bury and so she wasn't too keen on the idea. I said to her that, 'I'll never be able to make enough money to buy a house, or to do all the things that other people do who have good jobs.' She said that she didn't mind about that, so the months went by in my tedious job and I grew more and more frustrated. Eventually, one evening after an almighty row, I said, 'I am going to London. Either you come, or you don't.' And I set off there and then with a suitcase and what savings I had, London-bound. Was this the end of my marriage? Do I have to be an actor (no turning back now!)? How to keep depression at bay? Is it all just a pipe dream? These questions were going round and round in my head as the train slowly pulled out of Manchester Piccadilly station.

I soon managed to find and rent a relatively cheap room in Hampstead, in a big musty house. For my money I got a room with a bed and a boiled egg and toast for breakfast each morning. A week and a half passed before Sue wrote to me and said she was coming to join me, which made me happy, though I was also worried about how I was going to look after her in the big city. I met Sue at King's Cross and we got the tube to Hampstead, chatting about this and that, or was it that and this? The woman who made our boiled egg and toast would often spit in the sink while she was preparing breakfast, so we very quickly decided we had to get out of there. It wasn't just the lack of basic hygiene that was the problem: the whole place had an unpleasant and dark atmosphere. No wonder it was cheap!

I signed on the dole again and luckily we found a little guesthouse in Golders Green and the owners were prepared to let us have quite a large bedsit for free, in return for preparing continental breakfasts and being housekeepers. There were only nine rooms and it seemed ideal. I could prepare breakfast and do the housekeeping, while Sue got herself a job at Hampstead Royal Free Hospital, doing her silver service waitressing in the staff restaurant. She would serve lunch to the cream of London's medical profession. I would fill flasks with boiling water and put tea, coffee, toast, butter, marmalade and jam, plus a bowl of cornflakes, onto trays and place them outside each room.

We hadn't been living there long when I saw an advert in *The Stage*. David Halliwell, the writer of *Little Malcolm and His Struggle Against the Eunuchs*, which had been a hit play a few years earlier, was looking for actors to appear in an improvised play. I had never met him, but we had the same surname, and I wondered if this was some kind of sign. I telephoned the advertised number and arranged an interview. I told him about my life and my short acting career and the subject eventually turned to our mutual surname. In the end we agreed that

Halliwell was a Lancashire name, not a Yorkshire name. As David was a dyed-in-the-wool Yorkie, he was a bit put out at having to accept he had a name from 'ower t' top'.

He had several other actors and actresses to interview and so I left, not knowing whether or not he was interested in me, as he had given nothing away. I had pretended I had seen his famous play, but at that time I hadn't. Maybe he had realised I was lying about this? Days passed and fingernails were bitten as far down as they possibly could go. I ran out of patience in the end and decided I would ring him, rather than wait to be contacted. I think this gave him the impression that I had other work to go to and that I needed to know exactly where I stood, which could have put him off, I suppose. But when I told him that I would love to work with him if he thought I was right for the part he had in mind, he seemed to warm to me and gave me the job. I had only been back in London for a few short weeks and already I was working with a very successful and fashionable writer. Susie Figgis was in the cast – the same Susie Figgis who would go on to become a world-renowned casting director for many big and successful movies.

We eventually put together a play called *Minyip*, which was about an attempt to form a commune. I played a welder from Bury, a character based on my old mates Hardy and Dougy. We performed the play on the South Bank, in a small building on the site which became the focus of Sam Wanamaker's dream to rebuild the Globe theatre. Hardly anyone came to see it, but the play received favourable reviews, one in the *Financial Times*. I still have the pink paper-cutting of the review somewhere.

We immediately began work on another improvised play and Robin Carr was in the cast. He was an all-rounder of note – an actor, successful stage manager and eventually a successful producer too. The play was called *A Process of Elimination* and it was a long, rambling story, the exact details of which escape me. I had created a character that was, I think, totally unbelievable. I was playing a Cambridge student who was writing a book about how jazz music originated in England. How on earth I came up with this idea, I will never know, but I think it was my attempt to be funny. However, it didn't work. Robin had a speech that must have lasted for at least half an hour, consisting of lots of facts and details that no one could possibly follow, or be interested in. Only David, the director, thought it was a good idea.

At the end of Act One my character found a woman dead and I had to hold her wrist and say out loud, 'She's dead.' I argued and fought with David over this, asking if anyone would say 'she's dead' in such circumstances. I asked if I could say 'Oh God' or 'Oh no' instead, because the opening scene of Act Two was set in a coroner's office and the audience would immediately know that she had died. However, David insisted, saying, 'I want you to say, "She's dead."' And that was that. I wish he had listened, as one of the reviewers said my delivery of that line was the worst bit of acting he had ever seen.

Mike Leigh, the famous director who would go on to create *Abigail's Party*, *Nuts in May* and a string of award-winning films, came to see the play as he was a friend of David's from RADA. If I remember correctly, his then wife, Alison Steadman, a famous actress in her own right, was with him. Mike's comment on the play was, 'You have committed the cardinal sin in the theatre, David.'

'Which is?' asked David.

'You bored us,' said Mike.

It had been a good break meeting David Halliwell and working with him, but now I had bored Mike Leigh, which was definitely not a good career move.

David had been doing improvised plays simply because he was suffering from writer's block, which was a phrase I hadn't heard of until then. I would go out drinking with him maybe once a week on average and if I had no money he would pay.

He was a kind man. He had suffered a nervous breakdown and as a result of this, or perhaps it was just one of his eccentricities, he had a peculiar habit. When walking with him he would suddenly speed up to at least double the previous pace and I would really have to stretch my legs in order to keep up. Then, just as suddenly, he would slow down again. I never broached the subject of this oddity, but it was sometimes difficult not to laugh. I performed some of his sketches in pub theatres and, eventually, inspired by David, I began writing for the stage myself, in order to try to add another string to my bow.

We hadn't been in Golders Green very long when I got a job in Newcastle. David knew I was struggling to get work and so he recommended me for the small part of Cardinal Richelieu and that of a jailer in John Whiting's *The Devils*. This meant that I had to leave Susan behind in London, where she would have to do two jobs: breakfasts at the guesthouse and her daytime job at the Hampstead Royal Free. I felt terrible, but I knew that the acting job would only last for a few weeks.

The Tyneside Theatre Company was based at the university in Newcastle and as I watched the students lolling about on the grass, laughing and generally enjoying life, I felt quite envious. How wonderful it would have been if I had been able to get a grant for a full-time drama course. Of course, in those days it was possible to get grants from the local council if qualifications for university or drama school were gained, but I wasn't aware of this when I was at Mountview. With hindsight, I should have got myself auditions at the major drama schools. If I had been accepted, I may well have succeeded in getting a grant from Bury Town Council. I cannot be certain of this, but, anyway, it was all too late for that by then.

The weeks went quickly and I was soon back in London with Susan. Because she had had so much to do in my absence, she had become very fatigued and had overslept one morning, failing to do breakfast for the guests. She had been warned by the proprietors that if this happened again we would be sacked. I felt terrible that I hadn't been there to help, yet I still felt that pursuing an acting career was the right thing for me. If ever I was to make a decent living, I was certain that it would be as an actor.

When I met up with David Halliwell again, he told me that he had received a play which had been smuggled out of prison. The play was written by George (known as Gus) Thatcher, who, I believe, was the last person in this country to be locked in the death cell. He wanted David to work on his play and produce it. It was all part of his plea of innocence and was set during the three weeks he spent in the death cell prior to his appeal. He had been convicted of a murder committed during the course of an armed robbery, but, while admitting that he was a career criminal, he said that he hadn't even been present at that particular job. His pleas of innocence, however, had fallen on deaf ears and in those days the penalty for murder was usually the death sentence.

The play was called *The Only Way Out* and David did indeed begin working on it, polishing it for production and asking me if I wanted to be involved. I was hoping he would ask me to play the central character, Redmond, and I felt a sudden urge to tell him that I had been in prison myself. But, before I had a chance to blurt out this regrettable part of my life, he told me that Michael Elphick was to play the part. Michael, of course, later became famous for several TV roles, especially in *Boon*, which was a very popular series. I was to play the part of Tom, a prison officer who was integral to the story, meaning that I would be on stage for the duration of the play.

We first performed it at the New End Theatre, Hampstead, and it received some very good reviews. Such success, however, came at a price, for I had to leave Susan behind again while we toured various arts venues up and down the country. When the tour was over, I wasn't sure what I should do. I didn't want to go back to manual work, but at the same time I couldn't leave Susan to be the breadwinner, so in the end I got a job with Kensington and Chelsea Council. Autumn had set in and my job was to drive a little truck around and pick up plastic bags full of fallen leaves, which I then took to the tip. Part of my round included Sloane Square and I would stare across at the Royal Court Theatre and dream of one day performing there. Only a few months passed before my dream became a reality as *The Only Way Out* was given a production at the upstairs venue.

By the time the play was performed there, Michael Elphick was filming a television series and so was unable to play the part of Redmond. An actor called Brian Croucher took over the lead role and really made it his own. Harold Hobson, the highly respected *Sunday Times* theatre critic, came to see the play and he gave it a rave review. In fact, this was the last review he ever wrote, just before his retirement. Now some of the Sloane Rangers, who had ignored my existence when I was picking up leaves around the square, were actually paying to see me perform, as well as the other actors of course. Harold Hobson's review, which included my name, was blown up and posted outside. It almost took my breath away to see my name in big lettering outside the Royal Court Theatre. The play then went on to win the Arthur Koestler Award, which meant that I was now achieving both critical and artistic success, which was a great thrill. However, I was still poor materially and after the play closed it meant that I headed straight back to standing in line at the dole office.

Susan had been working hard and had been able to save quite a bit of money, so she headed back to Bury for a two-week holiday and to visit her parents. I couldn't go with her, simply because I was tied to doing breakfasts at the guesthouse. One night whilst she was away, I went for a night out with David Halliwell and once again the wine and whisky took its toll, resulting in my oversleeping and missing putting out the breakfast trays. I was told by the owners of the guesthouse that we would have to get out. I asked for some time to allow us to find new accommodation, but I was heartbroken that, on her return, I would have to tell Susan that we had nowhere to live. As luck would have it, one of Susan's friends from work came to the rescue, telling us we could have a free room in a flat owned by one of her relatives if we would look after him, as he was an old gentleman. He was a medical librarian at St Thomas's Hospital and was very old and frail, but was still working. We had to cook for him and keep him company in the evenings. We agreed to do this and I did most of the caring for him, as Susan was still busy working at the hospital.

Meanwhile, I continued signing on and looking for acting work, though I fervently hoped finding work would be easier now that I had an agent. Libby Glenn had come to see the play during its run at the Royal Court and had been quite taken by my performance, so she signed me on to her books. This meant that there were now two of us looking out for work and so, surely, I had double the chance of finding it. Libby was an American and she had been an actress herself, so I was thrilled to be represented by her. Now I felt like the real deal. I had appeared at the Court and I had a London agent.

David had managed to free himself from the torment of writer's block and had written a TV play for a series called *Second City Firsts*, which was being produced at the BBC in Birmingham. To my great surprise and delight, he had written a small part specifically for me. It was to be directed by Alan Dosser, who had been the artistic director of the Liverpool Everyman Theatre, but had now moved into television. Bernard Hill was to play the lead role. Bernard later made a big impact with his portrayal of Yosser Hughes in Alan Bleasdale's magnificent *Boys from the Blackstuff*. Alan Dosser had worked with him in the theatre, in the Everyman's *Halcyon Days*, alongside actors such as Julie Walters, Pete Postlethwaite and many others who would go on to enjoy successful and distinguished careers in both film and television. The short play of David Halliwell's was called *Daft Mam Blues*. Bernard Hill and I were about the same age, but he was a very confident young man, whereas I was a very insecure one. I needn't have worried though, as everything went well and I now had a television credit to add to my CV.

We had only been living with the old gentleman for a short time, perhaps a couple of months if memory serves me well, when we received a phone call informing us that he wouldn't be coming home as he had been taken seriously ill and was to remain in hospital for the foreseeable future. It was only about a week later that we received the sad news that he had died and so Susan and I wondered what on earth we would do now.

Susan found some accommodation for herself at the Royal Free Hospital nurses' quarters, and so we decided that, once she was safe and secure there, I would find us somewhere else to live. I went back to the old gentleman's house one evening and the door was bolted. I knocked and the landlord answered. He was a 6-foot-something Irish builder and, unbeknownst to me, he had wanted to get the old gentleman out so that he could sell the house. When I tried to pass him in the hall he asked where I was going (though not in such polite terms!) and I said that I was going to the flat. He remonstrated with me, telling me that I didn't live there, but I reminded him that we had been caring for the old gentleman. In the landlord's eyes because the old man was now dead he refused to accept that I had any right to be there. When I persisted in trying to get past him, he grabbed me by the throat and pushed me up against the wall. Fortunately, his wife appeared and this big Irish builder suddenly turned into a small timid boy. 'Pat,' she said, in rather a firm tone, and his head went down, his huge frame seemingly shrinking along with his once tough demeanour. He then let go of me and shuffled away sheepishly.

I explained to his wife that Susan had already left and that I was there to pick up my belongings, but, before I could finish explaining, big Pat reappeared and he pushed me out through the door with such force that I fell down two steps, landing painfully on my back. The door was then slammed and I could hear them arguing inside. And then all fell silent. What to do? What do you think I did? I headed for the pub and had a few pints, while I thought about how to get my things out of that house with an aggressive Pat looming large inside. I wondered if I should try again, hoping they would be reasonable. All I owned would fit in one suitcase. So I headed back to the house, but by now it was quite late and they could well have gone to bed so I was reluctant to knock on the door. I was determined not to be beaten, however, so, on noticing a slightly open sash window in our ex-flat, which happened to be close to a drain-pipe, the solution was obvious. I clambered up it and got in through there. I then decided not only to recover my belong-ings, but to actually sleep there that night. That's shown you, Big Pat! I thought as I got my head down to dream. I quietly left in the morning: the end of yet another era.

I still had quite a bit of money left over from the TV job, so I went in search of a bedsit, hoping I could find somewhere affordable in a nice area of London. I wandered around Belsize Park and eventually noticed a scrap of paper in a window announcing, 'Room to Let'. I knocked on the door and was promptly shown to what had been the cloakroom of the original house, with the clothes pegs still in it. It had a single bed, a wooden chair and no cooking facilities, but the upside was that it was cheap and somewhere to rest my head until we could find somewhere better. There was a payphone in the hall, so Libby could get in touch if she succeeded in get-ting auditions for me. In those days, of course, there were no answer machines, which meant that Libby couldn't leave any important messages, so I would telephone her every couple of days to see if anything had turned up. More often than not, nothing had.

David Halliwell rang me one day and said that he and a few friends were putting on a production of Ionesco's *Rhinoceros* at the Little Theatre in St Martin's Lane and that, if I was interested, there was a small part for me. Mike Leigh was also in the play, having the part of the Logician. Richard Ireson was to direct and the lead part was to be played by Michael J. Jackson. All of these people were much more experienced than I was and so, when I went for the first rehearsal, I just couldn't muster the courage to go in. It wasn't the acting that worried me: it was my lack of social skills. I kept wandering around Trafalgar Square, trying to gee myself up to go into the theatre. At least David Halliwell was also to act in the play, so I felt I had at least one ally. This gave me the courage to eventually overcome my nerves and we did the play. A talented young girl played the maid – her name was Celia Imrie and, as I am sure you are well aware, she would go on to have a very successful career, appearing in, among many, many other productions, *Calendar Girls* and the ever-popular *Darling Buds of May*.

During a night out with David Halliwell and a French writer and his wife, Susan was thinking to herself, What have I got myself into? Why couldn't I be with just some ordinary workman, and we could live an ordinary life? Why did this man want to be an actor? I didn't have the answer myself. I felt driven to do what I was doing and sometimes I felt like an unwilling participant. A lot of actors I have spoken to over the years also say that they feel driven to do what they do. Some even say that it is a calling, rather than a career, in much the same way as some nurses or priests feel they have a calling. I am not sure what I believe in that regard, but I certainly felt that I had no choice in the matter – that acting was what I was meant to be doing with my life.

Work in the acting profession wasn't very forthcoming and this meant that I was signing on the dole quite a lot. I didn't want to take yet another manual job, simply because I needed to be free to go to interviews and auditions. Libby sent me for a number of jobs, but I didn't get many of them. Another TV job did come along, however, this time for Granada: a small part in a dramatisation of the trial of Socrates. Socrates was to be played by the poet Christopher Logue. Although such parts gave me more much-needed experience, they hardly provided a living.

Susan and I had been seeing each other as often as we could and, although it was not strictly allowed, I had stayed overnight at the nurses' quarters on occasion, sometimes having to borrow money from her when out of work. Trying to live the life of an actor and that of a husband in London was becoming impossible. Susan, in the end, sadly decided she would return to live with her parents in Bury. I felt a complete failure. I was crushed, but still I could not give up on the idea of being an actor; of one day earning a decent living in a profession that I felt had been thrust upon me. I still felt driven to succeed. I had given it all up for Susan once, that is true, but that decision hadn't worked out for the good either, so I stuck with it. How was I to carry on? Once she had gone I often wandered the streets feeling very, very low.

One misty, rainy day while I was wandering, I bumped into an ex-Mountview student named Brian Davis, a lad from Swansea; he had also wanted to be an actor, though by then had given up on the idea. He was living in a single-room bedsit not too far away from where I was based and so we met up. The year was 1976, which is remembered for one of the hottest summers on record. The sun blazed down that year and the 'beautiful people' would gather around the ponds on Hampstead Heath – actors, models, musicians: people with time on their hands who were there to enjoy the sunshine and swimming in the ponds. Picnic baskets and champagne were a common sight. I recognised famous model twins and a few people I had seen on TV, but I could not put names to their faces. Brian and I would often be there, not as hangers on, or friends of anyone, but simply to try to catch their conversations. Quite a lot of public school guffawing would echo across the cool waters, where swimming was free, so we made certain we were not excluded from that part of the summer scene.

One day I took a pretty nifty little dive from the spring-board and it was so hot and lovely that I decided, once I was in the water, to take my trunks off and swim naked. After gliding around in the murky green water for a time, enjoying my nakedness, I put my trunks back on and emerged from the depths. I strolled back to where Brian was sunbathing and noticed that lots of girls were looking at me. Well, I was rather tanned and pretty good-looking, I thought, so why wouldn't those girls be looking over at me? I went into a strut-type walk I had learnt in movement classes, but when I got back to Brian and sat down I realised, to my horror, that I had put my trunks on inside out, which meant that I had a big piece of white gauze and string on display at the front, and a big pink label showing at the back. So those girls hadn't been admiring me at all, but had been having a good chuckle at my expense. That incident must rank as one of my most embarrassing experiences in life.

Brian told me that he had discovered a way of getting into a cinema at Hampstead without having to pay, which was something I was familiar with from when I was a lad back in Bury. This consisted of getting through the exit doors from the outside, though I think it best not to reveal exactly how this is done. So Brian and I would get in by this means and then walk up the exit steps into the bar, while discussing Fellini and Jean-Luc Godard, as if we were sophisticated cinema buffs, and the amazing thing was, no one ever questioned us. We watched the entire *Truffaut* season for free. Brian had many other methods of living a sophisticated lifestyle on very little money!

The Sir Richard Steele pub on Haverstock Hill, which was full of actors and boxers, was one of my favourite haunts.

I would sit in a corner and listen intently to the rather loud pontifications of Ronald Fraser, the film star. I would watch John Conteh, the World Champion boxer, swapping stories with his friends. I wanted so much to go over and buy him a drink, because I greatly admired him, but my financial struggles continued unabated.

Christmas Day came and I spent it alone, staring at an old flickering black-and-white TV that was perched on a chair. It had a bent coat hanger for an aerial. Christmas dinner was two cold processed pies, because, if you recall, I had no cooking facilities. I found it hard to cope with my situation, but I kept on repeating to myself, 'Nothing is going to stop me from being an actor.' I was glad of this resolve, because David Halliwell contacted me again some weeks later, and by then had been made the writer-in-residence at the Royal Court Theatre. He asked if I had written anything, as he was running workshops for new writers, and I said that I had – a play entitled *Where Are You Working Now?* David agreed to read my short play and decided that he would give it a workshop production. This meant that it would be read and polished by David and other writers and then would be given a one-off performance to a paying audience in the Theatre Upstairs at the Royal Court; that 'hallowed ground' had established the writing careers of John Osborne, Harold Pinter and many more, and was now going to showcase my first ever play. My main influences were Harold Pinter and Samuel Beckett, so the story was quite a bleak affair.

Brian said that he had enjoyed it, but that was about all he could say. It certainly wasn't Pinter, and who could out-do Beckett for sheer bleakness? I did feel a bit of an impostor and, had I not befriended David Halliwell, I don't think anyone at the Royal Court Theatre would have been interested in my play – having said that, it was still an amazing experience for a lad from Heap Bridge. After its debut at the Royal Court Theatre, my play went back to its usual place – at the bottom of my suitcase.

7

On the London Scene?

Zen is the game of insight, the game of discovering who we are beneath the social masks.

R.H. Blyth

Graham Cooper was an old mate from Bury who had grown up on what was known locally as the Dickie-Bird Estate, because all of the streets were named after different species of birds. Despite his humble background he was very clever indeed and had, after working for British Aerospace, become a teacher. He wasn't happy as a teacher, though, so he had become involved with Walter Kershaw, who was making a name for himself as an innovative mural painter. Walter had received several commissions for exterior wall decorations and Graham had helped out on these projects. He had then succeeded in getting a place at the prestigious Royal College of Art in London, on the strength of the community arts projects he had been involved with.

Graham and I would occasionally meet up and have a pint or two together, or sometimes we would go and see a live band. He told me there was a big party arranged at the student accommodation and he invited me along. The party was to take place in the cellar. I was quite envious of Graham during my visit, as he had a light and airy room in Kensington which was all paid for under the grant system. The atmosphere was good at the party, which was attended by the cream of young British artists, drinking wine and beer while enthusing mightily about their various projects. I got into a rather deep conversation with an American woman who I think was the partner of one of the college tutors. As the evening wore on, I began to feel that at last I was in some way involved in the creative, hedonistic lifestyle I had craved for so long.

At around midnight, or perhaps a little later, Graham felt he had had enough and was going back to his room. He said that I must remember his room number, as I was sleeping there that night and all the rooms looked exactly the same. I told him not to worry and that I would have no problem remembering his room number. And so Graham headed off, while I continued philosophising with the American lady. She had a deep, husky voice and I just wanted to listen to her talking, so I kept on asking her more and more questions. There had been plenty of free booze on offer, so I was rather drunk by this time, but, nevertheless, I turned and went over to the drinks table in order to get a refill. I asked the American if she would like another drink and she said no. When I came back, she had gone, no doubt tired of explaining every aspect of her life and philosophy to a complete stranger.

There were only three of us left at the party, so I decided that it was about time I headed to Graham's room for some much-needed sleep. Along the way, however, I suddenly realised that I couldn't remember his room number. I mulled over several possible numbers, but none rang a bell, so I decided that it would be a good idea to knock on a few doors in the hope that Graham would answer. It may be that I did knock on the right door that night, but Graham would undoubtedly have been well away and would not have heard me anyway. In the end I decided it would be best for me to try to get home, rather than keep knocking on doors that no one answered.

It was about four o'clock in the morning and my sense of direction, bad when sober, was almost non-existent. The last tube train would have long gone and I had no money for a taxi. I passed one of the kitchens on the way out and nipped in to have a look in the fridge. There were some bacon rashers in the fridge, so I grabbed some and put them in a plastic bag, and then stuck them out of sight down the back of my trousers. On the street I saw row after row of student bicycles chained to a fence. I hoped one would be unchained, as this could serve as my transport home. I was intent on only borrowing a bike, as I could return it when visiting Graham the next day. After a long search I found one with a chain attached, but it was not secured. I hadn't ridden a bike since I was a kid, but the old saying – that no one ever forgets how to ride one – proved to be true. But could I ride one in the state I was in? I hit a lamppost first and then went crashing to the ground – a hard pavement. I got up, got back on and rode a few more yards, thinking it a good idea to test the brakes, which resulted in me coming off again, this time over the handlebars. I had travelled for about 30 yards, if that, and had already fallen off twice, so I knew that this was going to be a long and arduous journey.

Whilst trying to get my bearings as I rode along the pavement, I came to the entrance to a park and thought it must have been either Hyde Park or Green Park, so I cycled in, trying to figure out the best way to make for home. I had just gone into the park through some large gates when I heard a voice shout, 'Stay exactly where you are.' Instead of doing as I was told, I turned and cycled out of there as fast as I could go, heading across the deserted road and, once well away from the park, I put the cycle in a shop doorway and walked nonchalantly on my way. I had only gone a few yards when two police cars screamed up beside me and I was then pushed against a wall. 'You were just on a bike, weren't you?' one of the officers asked. 'No, not me pal,' I replied. Surely all of this fuss wasn't over a stolen bicycle? I began to imagine that someone must have been murdered nearby and that I was going to get the blame for it. Then one of the officers walked back along the road and found the bike I had so swiftly abandoned. 'It's here,' he shouted.

Down at the police station, I woke with an officer poking me and shouting, 'Are you f****** listening?' I had fallen asleep during their interrogation and still didn't know what on earth all of this was about, so I was refusing to say that it was me they saw on the bicycle. Then they informed me that I had ridden into the grounds of Kensington Palace and that the voice shouting, 'Stay exactly where you are' was that of one of the many officers who had been pointing guns right at me. It was the time of the IRA bombings which were rife during the 1970s and as far as they were concerned I could have been a terrorist intent on planting a bomb. So I told them the story of how I had come to be cycling home after a party and that I had missed the last tube train home, so had borrowed a bike, but was planning to take it back the following morning. They didn't seem too convinced, however, so they locked me up anyway. I didn't protest, as I wanted desperately to get some sleep and shake off the hangover from that evening's celebrations.

As I was handing over my belongings, including my shoelaces and belt so that I couldn't hang myself, I remembered the bacon down my trousers. I hoped they wouldn't find it, as I hadn't a clue how I would explain that one away! The officer then asked me to raise my arms and began frisking me, patting down my body in search of knives, guns or any other weapon I may have been concealing, and then he felt the plastic bag. I could see by the smug look on his face that he thought he had found some sort of explosive and he pulled out the package, laid it on the desk and began to open it carefully. Both the officers were doing their best to keep as far away from it as possible, as though they were in imminent danger of being blown to pieces. Then, on at last getting the package open, both officers looked at each other, at the bacon, then at me, with looks of total disbelief. I almost burst out laughing, but thankfully managed to stop myself.

I was probably going to be charged with stealing a bike, but didn't want to compound the situation further by telling them I had stolen the bacon too. I simply told them that I had intended the bacon to be my contribution to tomorrow's breakfast, but they didn't really believe me. Neither could they come up with a solid case of theft – it was a ham-fisted attempt at real police work!

They released me the following morning and told me to return for formal charging. This may have been in order to give them time to investigate further, no doubt to see if they could connect me with the IRA. May I take this opportunity to apologise to both the owner of the bacon and the bike, as the police never did discover who the real owners of either of them were. When I eventually appeared in court, the magistrate didn't seem too pleased with the police wasting his time with such a trivial matter as borrowing a pushbike. I explained that I had borrowed the bike with the intention of returning it, but still I was fined £15 for taking a bike without the owner's consent and then I was free to go.

I have always had a traditional view of the man's role in life: he should be strong and provide for his family. On the one hand I think the bravest men are those who do not need to resort to violence, yet at times it is extremely difficult to live up to that ideal. In a man's world, according to society's thinking, if a man doesn't stand up for himself then he will be bullied. This creates a dilemma for those who do not wish to be violent. At one time I made a bit of a reputation for myself after knocking out a couple of guys in Bury, but as far as being a good provider was concerned I was definitely at rock bottom.

In an ideal world, I would provide for a good woman and children, but I was still a long, long way from reaching that goal. Things did start to pick up, however, as I managed to get several more acting roles for television. I played a police officer in *Crown Court*, which was an incredibly successful daytime drama during the 1970s and '80s. I played a council official in *Coronation Street* and another police officer in *Pickersgill People*, which was written by Mike Stott. I met up with Bernard Hill again, who was playing the lead role in an episode in which I was also to appear. Roger Sloman, who had found fame in Mike Leigh's *Nuts in May*, Philip Jackson and Brian Pringle were also in the cast. I was becoming more confident as a television actor, but I felt that the parts were not really big enough to fully test my skills. Still, I was learning much by watching others perform at close quarters.

Mum was still living in Stamford and she was enjoying life again, having married Gerry, a retired potato wholesaler. My brother, Clive, had volunteered for submarines and he was part of the crew that created a world record by sailing from Singapore to Scotland without surfacing, in HMS *Valiant*; this trip would have been totally impossible for me as I would have found it a claustrophobic nightmare. My old mate Hardy had been doing the hippy trail and on his way back to England from Morocco, he was stopped and searched at Orly Airport in France. He was caught attempting to smuggle hashish and was later sentenced to eighteen months in prison. He was about to be released and decided he would visit me in London on his way home to Bury. I had been writing to him all the time he'd been inside. When he knocked on my door it was great to see him again and he told me all about his adventures on the road.

He had been as far afield as Australia, where he had stayed with some of his relatives. He also told me he had never eaten as well as when he was in that French prison and that he had enjoyed access to great literature. He had been reading the *I Ching* and had become a full-blown hippy, if there is such a thing.

I explained that Susan and I had decided to end our relationship and he was sad for me, asking why I didn't just give up on the idea of becoming a successful actor. 'I don't know. I just have to do it,' was all I could say in reply, as I didn't fully understand what drove me. We enjoyed a few beers in the evening and had a few laughs as we reminisced over old times. It was great spending time with an old mate, but all good things must come to an end and in the morning he was away, continuing his journey back home to Bury.

I began getting interested in Zen Buddhism and this led to me wandering around Hampstead Heath trying to reach and maintain a state of meditation, while saying a little poem to myself, which goes as follows:

Before the first step is taken the goal is reached.
Before the tongue is moved the speech is finished.
More than brilliant intuition is needed
To find the origin of the right road.

I wondered if my driven 'madness' to become a successful actor, and to continue on this course against all odds, and sometimes at great cost to myself and others, was in some way reflected in this poem. I felt that part of me had already reached that goal, in the sense that being an actor was what I was meant to do with my life; maybe we come on to the planet and certain tasks have to be accomplished before we eventually pass away. I was on the path, true, but I felt that a long journey was still ahead of me. Buddhists, of course, believe that we have many lives and that we should develop our higher consciousness in order to finally reach Nirvana. I had dabbled with other philosophies and even wondered if I would eventually end up becoming an atheist, but then, on reflection, I felt that this amazing universe and the amazing complexity of just our own single planet could not have happened just by chance. It is convenient to believe in Darwin's theory of evolution. Those who allow themselves to believe in 'the survival of the fittest' could feel they have a license to commit almost any crime they wish. The rich could squash the poor in the name of Darwinism.

8

Backward Journey

Conformity is the jailer of freedom and the enemy of growth.

> John F. Kennedy

While withdrawing money from the cash machine at my bank one evening, I realised that computers couldn't always give you the information you required late at night. The information I was seeking was how much money I had in my account. The computer simply stated that it couldn't provide such information, so I drew out £100, knowing for certain that I didn't have such funds in my account. I was behind with my rent at the time, so this money was part of a plan I had: to make my getaway from London. I hadn't had any work for some time and there seemed to be none on the horizon, so, during the early hours of the morning, I slipped quietly away and booked my place on a coach back to Manchester. My attempt to make it as a successful actor had failed, though I was determined that this was only a temporary setback.

When I arrived back in Bury, I went to the Rayners, a pub in the town centre. This had been a very trendy place during the 1960s and had even been frequented by the late, great George Best. An old mate, Dave Crook, was in there. I call him an old mate, but I didn't really know him that well. However, when I told him I had nowhere to stay, he offered me a room. Crooky, as we called him, had had a tough time of it as a young lad, losing his mother when he was still in his teens. His father wasn't on the scene either, so he and his brother inherited the house when they were only young. Dave bought his brother's half of the house and so, at only 17 or 18 years of age, Crooky was a homeowner, which was unheard of in those days. He played guitar, sang in bands, and looked like Roy Wood from *Wizard*. Thus he had become a bit of a celebrity in the town. He also hosted many mad parties and his house became known as the Fifty-Three Club.

One evening a gang of local rogues were back at the house and they asked what had brought me back to Bury. 'I've come back to try to sort my head out,' was my reply, which roused much laughter because I had a bottle of strong cider in one hand and a joint in the other. Whilst living at Crooky's, I had spells signing on the dole and spells doing manual work, as well as the occasional acting job. I appeared in *Coronation Street* again, this time playing a council official who was to throw Percy Sugden out of his flat. That didn't make me popular at all in the local pub and one bloke actually had a go at me. I explained that the programme was fictional and that I was acting a part, but there was no reasoning with the idiot. Though very tempted, I managed to stop myself from punching his lights out.

There were many a long night spent at Crooky's listening to the likes of Pink Floyd, Steely Dan and Robin Trower while sharing the occasional smoke or two. This was towards the end

1 Mother and father's wedding day, 13 April 1938.

2 My grandfather Fred Halliwell, the coal miner.

3 Grandfather Harold Moss, conductor and well-known bandmaster.

4 Left to right: Me, George, Jacko and Hardy in Torquay.

5 Left to right: Me (kneeling), David Crausby, 'Mad' Hardy, Dave Ogden, Bernard Haworth and, kneeling, Mick Douglas, enjoying the surroundings of industrial Bury. David Crausby is now Labour MP for Bolton North East.

6 Me being used as a prop for one of Hardy's performances in Kay Gardens, Bury.

7 When we were mods. Left to right: Dave Wood, George and yours truly.

8 The Saracens: Me, Paddy Kirwan and Dave Ogden.

9 Aged 17, shortly before going on the road and living rough.

10 Playing Bottom in *A Midsummer Night's Dream* at the Oldham Coliseum, April and May 1987.

11 Another shot of the same production (me on the right).

12 *Aladdin*, with the M6 Theatre Company.

13 In a production at the Little Theatre, St Martin's Lane, London.

14 'Mad' Hardy in his 'big underpants', looking very serious. Taken at Shepherd Street, Bury, in the 1960s.

15 Hardy about to reveal his 'big underpants'. Me in the foreground.

16 My first publicity photo as a professional actor.

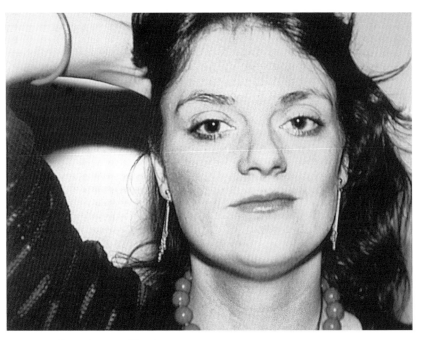

17 Valerie. I lost myself in those eyes.

18 Valerie with some of her paintings at the Globe Arts, Waterfoot, Rossendale, in 1996.

19 Back row: Me and Judith Barker. Middle Row: Eileen O'Brien, Tim Brierley, John Fraser, Brigit Forsyth, Joyce Kennedy. Front row: Michelle Holmes and Rachel James. From *The Practice*.

20 As Sam Renshaw in *Harvest in the North* at the Oldham Coliseum, September 1986.

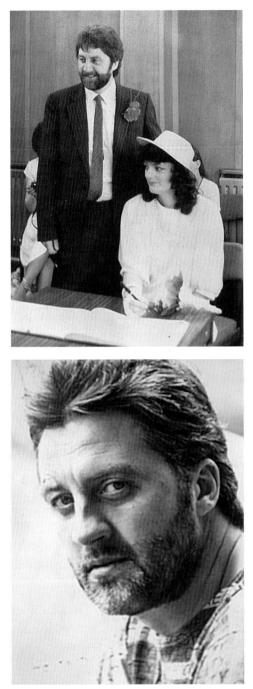

21 The two of us on our wedding day in 1984.

22 A photo taken by Valerie in 1984.

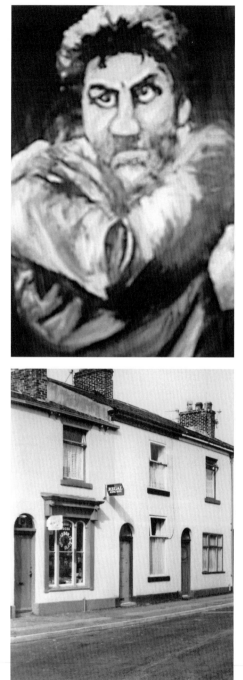

23 Valerie's take on my mad side.

24 Our first home (middle door), Manchester Old Road, Bury, 1982.

25 Happy times with my daughter, Charlotte. Westgate Avenue, Bury.

26 Our house at Clarence Street, Burnley (now demolished).

27 Valerie's final outburst in *Brewing Up*. Derby Hall, 1981.

28 The opening night of *All My Joy* at the Bury Metro Arts Centre.

29 Happy on our wedding day.

30 Left to right: John (Val's son), Valerie, Nicholas (Val's son) and cousin Katie. Charlotte is in front of Valerie. Bury, 1984.

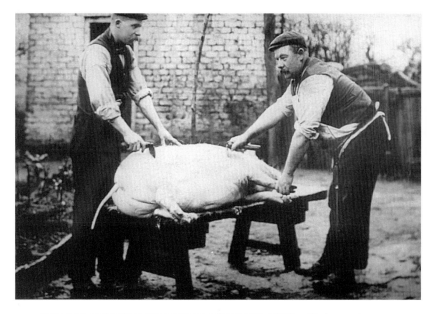

"A SHOW NOT TO BE MISSED"
Manchester Evening News

"SHEER EXUBERANCE"
The Independent

"SUPERBLY IMAGINATIVE"
The Guardian

"A MAGNIFICENT JOYOUS SPECTACLE"
Manchester Evening News

A MIDSUMMER NIGHT'S DREAM

by William Shakespeare **Oldham**
C O L I S E U M
━━THEATRE━━

BOX OFFICE
061-624 2829

"FUN AND ENJOYMENT"
Oldham Chronicle

"IT CASTS ITS DREAM LIKE SPELL"
The Guardian

'IF IT DOESN'T MAKE YOU LAUGH, YOU'RE ALREADY DEAD"
The Independent

ENDS JUNE 6th - BOOK NOW

31 A recently discovered photo of Great-Grandfather Moss, who was a butcher and who probably farmed pigs and other livestock. Does the cap look familiar?

32 A programme from the Oldham Coliseum when I appeared in the featured play, with excerpts from some excellent reviews.

of the 1970s and a lot of people had burnt out because of over-indulgence in drink and drugs. Some people I had known were dead. The George Hotel, another town-centre pub, had now become the trendy place to be and it was frequented by several characters, some of whom I knew from the past, and some whom I would come to know as friends.

I saw Susan again, but we didn't take up where we left off, as she had a new boyfriend.

I got behind with my rent at Crooky's quite quickly as work was rather thin on the ground. Crooky was about to embark on his own travels abroad and as luck would have it I got a TV job and was able to pay back all the rent arrears. He was happy for me to keep living there, as he knew I would look after the house while he was away. Not a lot of acting work was coming in, so I took a job with the local council, working in the parks department.

A lot of the characters frequenting the George Hotel had nicknames, which were earned in lots of different ways. For instance, if someone bobbed their head round the door and asked, 'Is Donald in?' someone would always ask, 'Donald in the Corner?' or 'Donald Nose?' There was Fierce Pete, who was also known as Peter Mustard or Peter MacMustard. This became Pedey MacMustard, and then eventually morphed into Pierre Moutard. Crooky also had several nicknames, including Cruikshanks, Sheepshanks and Nine-eyes. There was also 'Cobo', real name Anthony Cohen, who was a ginger, jockey-sized super clown who loved horses; betting on them, that is. One particular Saturday afternoon, Cobo was walking through the pub with the *Racing Post* sticking out of his back pocket, when someone thought it would be an amusing idea to set fire to it. Unaware of what was going on, Cobo carried on with the paper now well alight and so someone threw a pint over him to put it out. As Cobo didn't know why he'd been doused in this way he picked up someone else's pint and threw it over the offender. Bernard, the landlord, then barred him. Cobo pleaded with Bernard not to, but instead to bar the person who had set fire to his paper. He wouldn't listen and so Cobo was given the bum's rush.

I went into the George Hotel the following Saturday afternoon and Cobo was at the bar, pleading with Bernard to let him back in. 'Okay, just this once, but any more trouble and you're out,' said the landlord. Cobo was delighted and in celebration he shouted to the lads in the backroom, 'I'm back in lads. What are you having?' He bought a round of about eight pints of bitter and Bernard placed them on a tray. Cobo set off with the tray, but tripped along the way, spilling beer everywhere and smashing each and every glass.

'You're barred,' shouted Bernard.

'Oh, Bernard, it wasn't my fault – I tripped up,' Cobo replied, with a pleading tone in his voice.

'You're barred,' said Bernard again. The landlord then placed his arm around Cobo's little shoulder, not to console him, or to show any kind of sympathy, but simply to march him out the door, leading him outside before he had even had the chance to enjoy a single sip of beer. When he was eventually reinstated he was given his own man; a waiter would be allocated to follow Cobo, carrying his round of drinks on a tray to make sure they reached their destination.

Dave 'Ginger' Goodwin was living at Crooky's and then Tony, Crooky's older brother, turned up and he also ended up living there. Mick 'Dougie' Douglas also lived there for a short spell. On returning home from my work at the park there was sometimes a group of rogues, vagabonds and misfits all assembled at Crooky's, so it wasn't exactly the right environment for me when I needed to sort my head out. One night, after a heavy session on the drink, I gave my key to one of the lads, as he intended taking a girl back to the house. I returned at about three o'clock in the morning and knocked at the door, but no one answered. I then remembered the coaches lined up on the railway lines where we used to play as kids and decided that would be a good place to get my head down for what was left of the night. I made my way down the sloping bank towards the coaches parked on the sidetracks, but an 18-foot wire mesh fence prevented me from getting to my 'accommodation' – a fence which hadn't been there when I was a kid.

I used my drunken logic to figure out what to do and decided that I would just have to climb that fence. As I got to the top, the fence began to wobble violently and I slipped and fell head-first, but the back of my trousers caught on the wire and I hung there upside down 18 feet off the ground. I tugged and tugged and tugged until, at last, a tearing sound rapidly growing in tempo signalled that I was about to be set free. My trousers finally gave way and I fell onto the bank and rolled down until I was almost trapped between the bank and one of the railway coaches. I managed to get myself together and climbed inside. It was winter and extremely cold that night and I was covered in mud and snow from my fall. I was so cold that I couldn't sleep and then it dawned on me that I should have gone to Mark Gilman's, whose mother, Jenny, was always very kind to his friends. So that is what I did. I tapped gently on the door and eventually Jenny answered. She was shocked at my appearance and thought I had been beaten up, but I assured her I hadn't. I was too tired to explain just then, so she put a blanket over me and I told her about my nocturnal exploits in the morning.

I succeeded in getting a few more small parts on television, mostly at the Granada Studios in Manchester. Whilst there, I bumped into Michael Elphick, who was filming a popular series, and we went out for a drink together. As the evening wore on and the drinks began going down well, we decided to go and have a meal and were joined by Doreen Jones, head of casting, and Bill Gilmore, one of the directors of *Coronation Street*.

I felt somewhat out of my depth in such company and, due to jangling nerves, quickly drank too much, which resulted in me insulting Bill Gilmore. This would undoubtedly have ruined my chances of future work in *Coronation Street* so yet again my nervousness had led me to press the self-destruct button.

Derek Turner was a rather strange young man who hardly spoke a word, but he created beautiful drawings and paintings. Even on a one-to-one basis he would hardly speak, just nod or shake his head when asked questions. I was out with him one night and we went into the Royal Hotel in Bury; behind the bar was a very attractive young lady with long brown hair, a turned up nose, pale skin and the biggest, brightest eyes I had ever seen. 'Hello, Bambi,' I said as I ordered our drinks, and she smiled back at me. There was something familiar about her and I felt that she was going to be a significant figure in my life in one way or another, as if I had perhaps known her in a previous life.

Kev Jackson had moved to Summerseat, a little village on the outskirts of Bury, and from his garden we could watch the preserved steam trains chugging along the tracks to Ramsbottom and, ultimately, Rawtenstall, which really was like stepping back in time. Summerseat had been quite industrial in the past, but production at the mills had long ago ceased and they had now been converted into luxury apartments. Even the old rows of terraced houses built for the mill workers had been renovated and by then Summerseat was both a pleasant and trendy place to live. There was a large pub/restaurant there called The Waterside Inn and whenever I visited Kev we would go there for a drink and listen to live bands perform. Kev had returned to working in industry and had started to write poetry. He had written many songs in the past for his band Mobius Loop, but they had now disbanded.

Hardy had again set off on his travels and he ended up settling in Holland after marrying a Dutch girl called Jeannine.

He was living in Axel, which is close to the border with Belgium, to where he would travel to his work. George was living in Newquay and had married Mo, with whom he had a daughter. Occasionally Hardy would come over to England in order to visit family and friends, and George would sometimes come home at the same time. We would all meet up at the Waterside in Summerseat and so the old foursome – me, Kev, George and Hardy – would be together again. We would reminisce, telling again and again the same funny stories of our past adventures and the things that happened to us during that long, hot summer in Torquay. In the house where we had lived in Torquay, there had been a housekeeper called Rosie, who was painfully thin and more than a little dotty. One evening, Hardy realised that she had changed the linen on his bed and had replaced the sheet with a small tablecloth. This story still makes us laugh whenever we get together.

The Two Tubs in Bury was one of my favourite pubs and back in the 1970s it was considered the 'arty' place to be. Would-be writers, poets, artists and musicians would gather there. This was essentially a more middle-class scene, but there was a good mix of characters among them. Brian Harrison* was one of the leading lights at the Tubs. He was working-class, but not typically so. He was tall and thin with a longish beard, and had bridged the social gap by marrying an English teacher, Cath. They were the main bohemian couple of the town and Cath would put up with Brian staying at home all day, where he wrote poetry, read his books and drank his wine. They also lived in Summerseat. One hot summer's day Brian and Cath and a few of us drinking 'deadlegs' were sitting outside a pub when Cath suddenly said, 'I think it's so unfair that you men can just sit there without your tops on, and no one

---

* Note this name has been changed here and throughout to protect the individual's identity.

cares. It's not the same for us women.' Brian looked at her with total disdain and said, 'Why not take all your clothes off, Cath. I've always thought you looked perfectly adequate in a simple sanitary towel.' Brian eventually became a respected lecturer in English literature.

One of my favourite haunts in Manchester was the Band on the Wall. I would often go there for a drink and to listen to blues or jazz. I would mostly do this alone and drink a lot, when I had the coinage that is.

One Saturday night, after visiting a few musty pubs, I realised that I hadn't enough money left for my entrance fee for the club. I had supped the night away in my usual self-indulgent manner. So I headed for the bus station and sat down, looking back over my life. A clear realisation hit me hard. My dream of becoming a successful actor hadn't happened, and was likely never going to happen. My marriage was over, due to this crazy ambition, and the future looked devoid of sober happiness. What did it all matter anyway? I thought. The world could live without yet another poncey actor. Had all this just been an ego trip? I was filled with self-loathing and guilt, which made me wonder if I really wanted to carry on – carry on living at all, that is. Sinking lower, whilst drinking from a half bottle of whisky that I had intended to smuggle into the club, I prayed for help, and in the end must have lay down on the bench and dozed off into a fitful sleep. I became that familiar late-night city-centre character: The Drunken Bum. Remarkably my mood was gently eased, by some music drifting from the speakers around the bus station. Or, at least I think the music came from there: to this day, I am unsure whether it was real or imagined.

However, it sparked a question in my mind, 'Why are you sitting and waiting for work to come to you? You're an actor; you're a playwright – create your own work.' With this in mind I got a late-night bus home and the next morning went to meet Mark Gilman, a friend who had a lot of literary and political knowledge. Together we formed the idea of a community theatre group which would explore the problems of the unemployed. This was the era of the Thatcher government and at least 3 million people were out of work. Quite a lot of our friends had no jobs, and I was unemployed again myself. So we decided to write about people's real-life experiences and turn them into dramas, which we would then perform at the Derby Hall in Bury (today this building houses Bury Metro Arts).

The first play we worked on was one I pulled out from the bottom of my suitcase – *Where Are You Working Now?* One of the central characters was to be played by Stuart Warburton, who was a local guitarist and sang in his own band. We adapted the original script so that we could showcase one of Stuart's other skills, rockabilly double-bass playing. We also booked a band for the evening that the play was to be performed. Some who came were not initially interested in theatre but the prospect of seeing a live band would hopefully bring in bigger crowds. We called these 'gigs nights' and we kept the tickets cheap, which meant that they soon became very popular.

As I was the only actor with professional experience in the troupe, I would direct the play. Pierre Moutard's younger brother, Paul, performed in the first play and I acted in it as well. The barmaid at the Royal Hotel, Valerie, whom I had christened Bambi, was a regular at the George Hotel and we had become friends. There was a sadness about her that seemed familiar, something I knew I could relate to. She was going out with Mick Harlich at the time, who was an exceptionally gifted self-taught guitar player. The backroom of the George Hotel, in fact, was full of talented people.

Mark Gilman, the group's co-founder, worked for the drug rehabilitation project Lifeline, and eventually he would be asked to advise the then government on how to deal with the growing drug problems in society. His street awareness made him a valuable asset to any organisation that was intent on improving social problems, particularly amongst young people who had become involved with drugs. After the initial discussions, however, Mark didn't have much involvement in the theatre project, though he did later perform in one of the plays. We decided to call our little group the Interchange Theatre Project.

We worked in a very simple, yet effective, manner. People we knew in the pub would come up with ideas during normal conversations and some of these ideas we took on board, while others we rejected. The plentiful jobs of the 1960s were long gone and it had become more and more difficult to get even manual labouring jobs. Also, for me, the television work I had broken into seemed to have dried up completely.

Valerie's marriage had failed and she had ended up living on the Springs Estate in a flat, along with her two young boys, John and Nicholas. Susan and I had been apart for three years, and so we were divorced on those grounds. If I had been more successful as an actor, maybe our marriage could have been saved, but, as it was, it was now well and truly over. Most of my time living at Crooky's is a complete blur, not because I have forgotten as the years have passed, but because it was very much a blur at the time, marathon drinking sessions being the norm. One thing I do remember is that I was given two free tickets to an unknown club in Manchester and asked Valerie out on a date. She said yes. So we set off, anticipating a fun time together, but when we eventually found the place the doorman said, 'Shirt an' tie, pal. You'll need a shirt an' tie.' Valerie would have been happy just to move on and go somewhere else, but I didn't want to be beaten. I went to a café that was always open late and which was owned by a Greek family I had come to know quite well.

I asked one of the lads if he had a shirt and tie I could buy off him; he went into the back and came out with an old, folded white shirt and a piece of cloth that would serve as a tie. I gave him a couple of quid and off we went, back to the club. I went up a backstreet nearby and took off my T-shirt. As I opened the crumpled shirt, a cockroach the size of a buffalo ran straight across my hand. Val screamed and then we both burst out laughing hysterically. So, with my cockroach-infested shirt and a bit of dishcloth for a tie, we at last managed to get into the club, which was a sadly dull and dank place. This, my first date with Valerie, was obviously not as romantic as she or I would have wished. I don't think it put her off me, however, and we remained good friends for some time after that messy evening. We even spent one lonely Christmas together, platonically, as her relationship with Mick (the guitarist) was floundering due to his lack of commitment. This meant that, like myself, she was often at a loose end.

One evening, Valerie, over a drink, suggested an idea for a play based on some friends of hers who had suffered marriage problems due to unemployment and other factors. I would visit her flat and we would work together on a script. Val said she would also be willing to appear in the play and we talked Tony Gaffney, a local builder and member of a big Irish family, into playing the lead role. Jackie Benson, a friend of Val's who lived in a nearby flat, also appeared in the play. Completing the cast were Dave 'Ginger' Goodwin, Betty Douglas (Mick's mother) and me. This was to be the start of a long creative partnership with Valerie. She and I would go on to co-write most of the group's subsequent plays and she designed the sets for each production.

We would gather at Crooky's house or the back room of the George pub and read the lines, rehearsing over and over again. The group would then often say that they knew the script backwards, but I would always reply, 'One more time,' as I wanted to make certain that, no matter what else happened on the night, they would not forget their lines. Pete Brewer, Valerie's cousin, was a great guitar player and he had his own band, Opera.

They were to perform on the same night that we staged my and Valerie's first play, which was now called *Brewing Up*.

The play, in some ways, was about male domination and the oppression of women. Tony played a chauvinistic, football-playing, beer-drinking builder and in real life he was a football-playing, beer-drinking builder. Half of his family were in the audience, so he was very nervous before this first performance. As we stood in the wings waiting to go on, I could see real fear in his eyes. In the building trade at that time 'actor' was a term of abuse. It means you are not the real deal; you are not good at your job – 'He's not a bricklayer, he's an actor!' The house lights started to go down and the stage lights started to come up, and I could tell from his body language that he was ready to turn tail and run. The opening music started and I literally had to push him on stage, but then the endless rehearsals at last paid off. We quickly won the audience and began getting big, big laughs.

I was so proud of those first-time actors, who were instinctively pausing to allow the audience's laughter to die down, before carrying on with the dialogue. Then, close to the end, Val's character came to her big outburst. She really went for it and centuries of women's oppression were poured into those few climactic moments. The result, I am pleased and proud to say, was loud cheers and a standing ovation.

It had been a genuine theatrical experience for audience and actors alike. I think every woman in the room had felt represented by Valerie's final speech. We gave our last bow and then made for the bar. I said to Tony, 'How was that, pal?'

He thought for a few seconds and then replied, 'Better than being on acid.' All of us were as high as kites – not due to drugs or drink, but the heady and very sweet scent of success, something which had been rather elusive throughout my life. The theatrical hugs and kisses and the general bonhomie came naturally to all involved. The opening night of a play can be a magical experience, especially when the audience is won and goes home having thoroughly enjoyed themselves. The biggest buzz in show business for me comes from walking down stage for the final bow and hearing the applause and, if you are lucky, a few cheers. Theatre, as is true of television, is very much a collective art form and everyone involved in the success of a project is just as important as the next person. Incidentally, years later Valerie told me she had been embarrassed at receiving such cheers and applause for pretending to be someone else.

Whilst looking for rehearsal space at the Mosses Community Centre in Bury, I began chatting with Mike Twigg, who worked for the youth service there. I explained the concept of the Interchange Theatre (using local talent to produce plays and cultural evenings in and around Bury), and he told me there was money available for such schemes from the Manpower Services Commission. He asked how I would feel about working for them.

'What kind of job would it be?' I asked.

'You could create interest in theatre around the community. You could go into youth clubs and encourage an interest in the performing arts.' He went on to say that I would be based there, at the Mosses Community Centre and I said that I would be very interested in such a job.

From that one idea that came to me on a bus station bench in Manchester, I had a theatre project up and running, and now a full-time job. This taught me that you can make things happen, with determination and perseverance. All that we see happening around us in society was at one time just an idea and people have, with much hard work and determination, made it all a reality. If I had decided to end my life that night in Manchester, when all seemed lost, then I would have missed all the fun I was now beginning to enjoy, and much, much more yet to come. If this is true, that we do have the power to create our world, then let's make it a peaceful and caring one.

9

A Soul Mate, Perhaps

Life's most persistent and urgent question is, 'What are you doing for others?'
Martin Luther King

My relationship with Valerie had become much deeper than simple friendship and I often stayed at her flat. I had secretly fallen in love, but was fearful my love wouldn't be returned. We did everything together and in the local pub we soon became nicknamed Courting Couple. The Springs Estate, where she lived, had a reputation for trouble and the more I stayed there, the more I realised just how vulnerable she was in such a place. She was a young woman with two children and no one to help look after them. She once told me she had to drag an iron bar from a very aggressive woman and chase her off with it in order to stop herself from being bullied. Her two young boys, John and Nicholas, were aged 10 and 8 and I would often play football with them on a field by Valerie's flat, close to

Bury Football Club. I was certainly no professional, but, still, I could teach those boys a thing or two about the game.

After I had been at the Mosses Centre for a year or so, I persuaded the management to send me on a course for video production, as there was a lot of equipment at the centre that no one was using. The Youth Opportunities Programme was then in full swing and so many young people would come to the centre and I would work with them on drama and video production. I soon realised that every 'problem' lad and lassie was being sent to me, though I didn't really mind, because real opportunities were often denied them. At least they could have some fun in my classes.

I also ran classes for the MIND organisation; for people who suffered with mental health problems. It was interesting to see that none of these people wanted to go in front of the camera, except for one delicate, disturbed young boy, who asked to sing 'I Wanna Be Loved by You' – the result was incredibly moving to see and hear. Rehearsals for Interchange also took place at the centre and this was certainly an improvement on Crooky's living room, though it was still not ideal, as noise from other rooms in the building always interrupted our work. For instance, the Jazz Society often met next door. Not to play music, but to listen to records. It always seemed odd to me that they would listen to a full album, such as Duke Ellington, and then start clapping once it had finished.

I bumped into Barry Taylor* one evening at the centre. He was an older guy who was a steel fixer (making steel reinforcement for concrete) by trade and one-time 'champion boozer'. He had always been a big jazz fan and I asked if he was going for a pint after they had finished listening to the music. 'Not today,' he replied, so I knew he was off the booze. He once

---

* Note this name has been changed here and throughout to protect the individual's identity.

told me that his biggest fear with stopping drinking was that he might not like jazz, because, in thirty-five years of listening to it, he had never heard it sober. However, as he was attending the Jazz Society meetings, he was obviously still a fan.

I had had periods of stopping drinking myself, but always found it difficult to cut it out completely, possibly because it is so bound up with our culture. We drink for so many reasons: because we are happy, because we are sad. We drink because it's Christmas, or a birthday, or when we go out for a meal, or simply because it's the weekend. To stop drinking altogether almost felt like stopping eating. Most people in the Western world eat more than they need and I had certainly always drank far more than I needed. Even when I am aware that I have had enough, I still carry on, for some reason. The act of buying a drink and seeing it on the bar in front of me is all part of the joy, as is going to different bars, seeing different people and ordering different drinks. I missed these things when I stopped, almost as much as I missed the fake hazy happiness that alcohol induces. For me, drink deadened both mental pain and physical pain.

Val's flat was above another and we could often hear the potty family underneath arguing. It was the time when the CB Radio craze was sweeping through the country, during the 1980s, and we constantly heard things like, 'Come in, Cack String, this is Paper Bag, do you copy?' The lady downstairs called herself Paper Bag because she worked at Bibby and Baron's, which was a Bury factory where bags were produced in their tens of thousands. This wasn't really a very complimentary name, however, as it was commonly stated in Bury, after asking if a certain woman was attractive, that 'she's okay, but I'd have to put a paper bag over her head'. If a lad hadn't managed to pull a nice-looking girl by the end of the night he would go looking for a 'paper bag job'. At the Mosses Centre young girls would describe some boys as 'camels', so the insults cut both ways, it seems.

We would hear rows going on all the time in the flat below. One of the worst was when the loopy grandmother had lost all of the rent money on the horses. This was also one of the loudest and longest rows we heard. It went on and on. We would jot down a lot of what we heard, which we would then use for material in our next production. Val and I worked on a piece called *Is Nobody Listening*, which was based on this nutty and noisy family. We applied to North West Arts to see if we could get some funding and, after a long interview with me and a visit to see one of our performances, a small grant was awarded to our little theatre company. This was not enough to pay wages, but it at least gave us something towards expenses for room hire and publicity.

Meanwhile, Valerie and I grew ever closer and I eventually moved out of Crooky's and in with her and the boys, though a few times she threw my clothes out and down the stairs before I finally settled in and was totally accepted. This was on the understanding that I cut down on the drink. Ever since Susan had had the ectopic pregnancy, I had got it into my head that perhaps there was something wrong with my fertility, and though Valerie had enough on with her two boys, she said she wouldn't mind having another. And so, as I wanted to have a child before I was much older, we decided to try for a baby.

After I had got the job at the Mosses Centre, I had told Libby, my agent, that I was now in regular employment and would not be seeking work in television or theatre, so I was taken off her books. However, after a time, I began having pangs to be acting professionally again. Even though the work I was doing and the theatre projects we developed were very satisfying, I missed television work in particular. Having Val and the two boys to look after kept me busy, however. Sometimes we would all go to Ashworth Valley, which was, of course, an old haunt from my early days. We all enjoyed trekking along the river and picnicking. Also, John and Nick would have fun on a rope swing that hung from a tree in the middle of the woods. Whilst out there one Sunday morning, with the sunlight dancing across the river in silvery blades, I recalled past visits, such as the time Hardy and I had camped there in the old tent that I had kept since childhood.

One Friday evening we had got on to a bus bound for Heywood, intending to call in at a local pub just for a couple of pints before making our way to the valley campsite. But of course we drank and quaffed without let up, enjoying great laughs over the absurdity of our respective lives. We were quite shocked to hear the landlord bellowing, 'Time, gentlemen, please! Drink up!' And so we reluctantly upped sticks and left, gently staggering away into the night.

It was pitch-black by now and we had no torch, but I assured my mate that everything would be sound and that I could lead him safely to the campsite. Hardy looked doubtful to say the least, but nevertheless he followed as I led him into the darkness. 'I know these woods like the back of my hand,' I said. The journey would be about a mile and a half. After twenty minutes or so, we arrived at a particularly difficult and dangerous spot and I rather patronisingly said, 'Be really careful here, pal, follow my every step,' and then I was gone, tumbling through the bushes towards the river below. Somehow, despite the darkness, I managed to reach out and grab hold of a thick branch, which proved to be just in time, as there was a sheer drop to the river close at hand.

'Where are you?' shouted Hardy.

'I'm here, keep still or you'll end up down here with me.' Then I managed to slowly clamber back up the hill, covered in twigs and soil, to where he was waiting.

'What happened?' he asked.

'I must have slipped,' I replied, stating the blindingly obvious. We then carried on our way and eventually reached the clearing safely. Both of us had bought cans from the pub to round off the evening, which we began to drink, this being, in our culture, the macho thing to do.

My next conscious memory was of waking with the hot comforting sun on my back and the happy sound of children playing. All we had managed during the previous night was to put in one tent pole, and then we must have fallen asleep out in the open air, the empty beer cans strewn everywhere. The voices belonged to Cub Scouts who, with the assistance of their leader, had set up an entire camp while we slumbered. I could imagine the Scout leader pointing at us and telling the boys, 'That is how *not* to do it.'

We had brought some fish paste sandwiches and we ate them for breakfast, washed down with river water, which was much needed after our heavy session on the ale. We then made a little camp fire and whilst we both sat dropping twisted twigs into the flames, I heard a voice say, 'Ally?' This was my nickname, a shortened version of Halliwell. It was Barry Nicholson, my old mate from Heap Bridge. He was carrying a tent and a rucksack and was a most welcome sight, as I hadn't seen him for years. 'Alright, Nicky – are you doing a bit of camping?' I asked, thinking that that was the obvious conclusion.

But he replied, 'No, I'm on the run from the army.'

I didn't even know he'd joined up. He explained how oppressive the army had been due to his reluctance to obey orders, and Hardy and I just nodded in agreement, understanding his plight. He had been serving at Blackdown Camp in Hampshire, working as a stable-hand at a joint army and civilian stables. For some reason he kept being refused promotion and eventually decided he had had enough. He then went AWOL and was on the run. He did eventually give himself up at Bury Police Station and was given twenty-eight days imprisonment. Afterwards he was posted to Germany and he remained there until he had completed his six-year commission.

I had almost given up on the idea of fathering a child when one day Valerie told me that she was pregnant. I was totally and utterly thrilled. Val was hoping for a girl, but I didn't mind either way. I was going to be a dad! A father, me! At the time, we were working on our next production, *The Bicycle*. This play was set in Kay Gardens, an area right in the centre of Bury. In this piece, an old bicycle had been abandoned. Speculation regarding its ownership was the main theme, which was to be discussed by a group of 'misfits' sitting around in the gardens waiting for the pub to open at eleven-thirty in the morning. We had rehearsed the play over and over again, but had left a gap, so that Mark Gilman's character could put in an appearance, as he wanted to rehearse his long monologue by himself. He was to play Mad Morris, who was based on a real-life character in the town known as Mad Harold. This poor chap had suffered a nervous breakdown of some sort and it was sadly hysterical, listening to his crazy imaginings. Valerie was to make a guest appearance and I also appeared in the play. Mark's performance got a standing ovation after giving a fine portrait of free association lunacy.

As I was now in regular work and we were building up some savings, we decided to buy a house. Valerie had enough money for the deposit, which she had saved from the sale of a house after her past marriage had broken down. We settled on a little terraced cottage on Manchester Old Road. I liked it because it was near to the Rose and Crown pub. Valerie would have preferred a bigger terraced house. The proximity to a pub was of no interest to her, though she did eventually start working as a barmaid at that very same boozer. The house consisted of one room and a kitchen downstairs, and two bedrooms and a bathroom upstairs, with a yard at the back. We were under some new pressure now, as we wanted to move in before Val had our baby. One evening, tired after I had finished work, I was sitting staring at nothing in particular when Valerie suddenly said, 'You want to go back to being an actor, don't you, Steve?'

I thought for a minute and then said, 'Well, I have a regular job, so I can't take that risk again.'

'Yes you can,' she said. I told her that I was okay and that I felt I had lost my confidence as a professional actor, anyway. But she encouraged me to telephone Libby Glenn and ask her to put me back on her books.

'But you're about to have a baby: I need a regular job. You know what it's like in the acting game – in and out of work all the time,' I told her. But she said again that she could see part of me wasn't happy. So, in the end, I decided to phone my ex-agent and she invited me down for a meeting.

Val came to London with me. Her sister, Rosalind, had agreed to look after the boys, so we enjoyed a little break on our own. Libby's office was close to Charlotte Street and this, we decided, would be a good name for our child, if the baby was a girl. My nerves were bad and Val had to literally hold my hand as we crossed the street and went into Libby's office. I shouldn't have worried though, as the meeting went really well. Libby believed in me and must have thought that I could earn her some money, after all. She stressed that if she did put me on her books again, I had to be prepared to take any job that came along. I agreed to her terms and was back in the business of acting.

Back home in Bury, we still hadn't managed to get everything sorted with the house before Val went into labour. The drama of birth is something incomparable to behold, yet an every-day occurrence at the same time. The experience left a lasting impression on me. I had never before seen the sufferings of a woman in labour and I felt completely hopeless and helpless as I sat by her. All I could do was to hold her hand and stroke her head. But I shall never forget the delight on Valerie's face and the sound that she made when I said, 'It's a girl!' The sounds of suffering turned to sounds of joy. 'I've got a girl, I've got a girl,' Val said, seemingly in a state of bliss. I wrote a little poem after this mystical experience:

There were three people in a room,
My wife, the midwife, and me,
And then, there were four,
Even though no one had come through the door.

I immediately fell in love with our little daughter, but, just as immediately, I felt the weight of responsibility land on my shoulders with a heavy thud. We did name her Charlotte and, sadly, as was common in those days, she developed jaundice. She had to have a lamp placed over her and lots of other jaundiced babies were getting the same standard treatment. When I visited Val one evening, I was chatting away when she suddenly said that she could hear Charlotte crying. I thought she was just imagining it was our girl, but when we got to the room where the babies were, there was indeed only one child crying – our Charlotte.

It was November and the weather was very cold, so Valerie had to stay in hospital for a few extra days so that I could get the heating on in our new house. I was sleeping there already, with piles of blankets over me, as there hadn't been any heating on for months. The boys were being looked after by Rosalind, but after a couple more days, everything was sorted out and we at last moved into our new home. We had only been living there a few months when we were robbed. Our video recorder was stolen, which had in it a video of baby Charlotte and the boys, plus some short dramas we had made with the kids. I'd captured them on a video camera I had borrowed from the Mosses Centre. This meant that precious memories were gone forever. We didn't care much about the recorder, but the recordings were irreplaceable.

I was still working at the Mosses Centre when I got a phone call from Libby, saying she had got me an interview for a Christmas special of *All Creatures Great and Small*, which was an incredibly popular series at the time and is still regularly repeated on television. I was to audition for the part of

PC Goole, who was a comical country policeman. During the interview, I explained that I had been writing for theatre and acting with the Interchange Project and said I was wondering if I might move more into the writing side of the business.

They seemed interested in our project, but then asked me what it was I really wanted to do. I replied that I would like to be a successful actor. The director looked over at the casting lady, and then back at me. He said that he could offer me the job and the casting lady agreed. I was handed a script there and then – the job was mine. I quickly found a telephone box and rang Valerie. 'I've got it, I've got it!' I shouted, too loudly as it happened, which startled a passer-by.

Val shouted at me, 'Well done lad, well done!'

Then it was back on the coach for the long ride home. By the time we pulled into Piccadilly coach station in Manchester, some seven hours later, I had learnt the PC Goole part backwards.

This job felt like a real breakthrough for me; like fate had dealt me a good hand for a change. I decided to tell the management at the Mosses Centre that I would be leaving, so that I could concentrate on my acting career. They were disappointed at the news, but wished me well and, in some ways, I was sad to be leaving them. Still, onwards and upwards. I was very excited as I set off to Richmond, North Yorkshire, the location for the sequence I was to be involved with. *All Creatures Great and Small* legends Peter Davison, Christopher Timothy and Robert Hardy were all very easy to get on with and I had a really enjoyable and interesting time making that show and studying the different ways these actors worked. However, after it was all over and my head came back out of the clouds, I realised the TV work had disappeared once more. I had to take a job with Mick the Brick, a bricklayer who lived nearby. I was to be his labourer and we worked through the night carrying out building alteration work that couldn't be done during daylight hours because the factory would be in operation then. The acting luck had vanished as fast as it had arrived.

I was soon worrying about our financial situation again and wondered if leaving the Mosses Centre had been a good decision after all. I loved acting, but once again it was the old money problems dominating my mind. Val told me to, 'Hang in there!', and that something else would come along. She seemed to have great confidence in me, which helped a lot.

Baby Charlotte would wake in the early hours every night and so both Val and I were getting very weary. One particular night, at around four o'clock in the morning, we put Charlotte in her pram and went out for a walk with her, in the hope that she would stop crying. It worked. In the darkness, we could see her little face peeping out and looking at the surrounding trees as we walked around the park. Valerie kept on telling me not to pick her up every time she cried, as eventually she would fall back asleep if we left her. But, as she was right by my side in her cot, I just couldn't help but pick her up and put her in bed next to us, which, I suppose, didn't really help. We were really starting to struggle, as the job with Mick the Brick had also come to an end. Sometimes, being a smoker, I would pick up fag ends as I had no money left for cigs when everything had been paid for. Telephone boxes and bus shelters provided the most-dry tobacco, as anyone who has been in a similar situation will be aware of.

Then one sunny, laburnum-yellow day, lady luck came calling unexpectedly. A new series called *The Practice* was being produced by Sita Williams for Granada Television and I was to audition for the part of Peter Bishop, a social worker who was attached to the medical practice, at the centre of the drama. I got the job! I think my youth work at the Mosses had helped swing it for me. The programme, set in a medical centre in Manchester, was to be a 'warts and all' look at a group of doctors. Brigit Forsyth was to star and her husband, Brian Mills, who had been instrumental in the early planning of the series, was to direct. John Fraser, the famous film actor, would also star and so I found myself in very interesting company. I was to appear in five of the six episodes. The drama-documentary style was ahead of its time: the storylines were hard-hitting – cancer, cot death and other tragedies featured – and the vulnerability of both doctors and patients.

The first episode I was involved in saw my character dealing with a mother and child and the harrowing decisions social workers often have to make, such as do you take a child away from its mother and to be put into care? These decisions have to be made all the time by social workers and the character I played brought it home to me just how difficult this must be. We only hear about the times social workers get it wrong, never when they get it right.

A friend of mine, Linda, the wife of Mark Gilman, was a social worker and she had to deal with a case where a woman said to her, 'If you take my children away from me, I will kill myself.' In the end, no doubt after much soul-searching, Linda decided that she had to take the children from her. They were placed in care and the mother, true to her word, killed herself. Linda has since died of cancer – God rest her soul.

After the first six episodes had been filmed, it was decided by the powers that be that the programme was too hard hitting for viewers so early in the evening. Mike Stott, who I had worked with on *Pickersgill People*, was brought in to lighten up the scripts. Brian Mills, the director, was very angry about the change to the style of the drama and he wanted nothing more to do with it. Thus the original six episodes were never broadcast. I could see it from the television company's viewpoint, as I myself would not have wanted to see all that sadness and suffering with each weekly episode.

Michelle Holmes was in the cast, playing a receptionist. She was just 17 and would eventually find fame in *Rita,*

Sue and Bob Too! Judith Barker, a stalwart of the Oldham Coliseum Theatre, and who played the wife of Ken Barlow of *Coronation Street* during the early days, played the head receptionist. Joyce Kennedy, landlady of the once-notorious Cardigan Arms in Leeds, played the role of midwife. I was thrilled when I was asked to stay on as part of the cast after the initial episodes had been scrapped, which meant that my contract was extended. With improved finances, we decided to move out of our tiny home and we found a three-bedroom terraced house. It had coloured leaded-glass windows and an overgrown rose garden at the back and a small garden at the front. It also had dark wooden panelling throughout and had hardly changed since it was built during the 1930s. We loved it. The boys shared a room, Charlotte had the box room, and Val and I had the main bedroom. We felt that our quality of life was improving day by day. I almost felt normal, living this conventional family existence!

Myself and the boys would play tennis in the park just outside our front door and little Charlotte, growing fast, would run around and pick up balls in the middle of the game. It was like having our own private tennis court. As Charlotte got older she was allowed to play in the park with her friends and do all of the normal things such as climbing trees, making dens among the rocks and pulling up handfuls of flowers for Mummy. We had a heavy knock on the door about that little incident. Val's sister, Rosalind, lived around the corner; her daughter, Katie, would also be in the park and so Rosalind kept a close eye on Charlotte. Valerie was a full-time mum so there was only my income to keep it all going. Running a home was, and still is, a costly affair, so we could not afford to buy and run a car.

Valerie, who had painted and drawn from being a little girl, had always wanted to study art and to try to get a degree, but as she came from a very poor family, such things hadn't been possible. She had always been very supportive of me and my career, so I felt that it was only right to try to help her fulfil her dreams too. She did A Level Art and then a full-time foundation course at Bolton, and then eventually applied to the University of Central Lancashire in Preston to do a Fine Art degree. She was accepted. Somehow, we juggled everything so that Val could go to Preston, but she had a lot of homework to do in order to achieve her dream. After much heartache, tears and arguments, it all paid off as she succeeded in pocketing a Fine Art BA honours degree. Our busy schedules meant that Valerie and I could no longer devote time and energy to the Interchange Theatre and so sadly this part of our life came to an end, as did the theatre group itself. The project had been such fun. Even now we feel a sense of sadness and nostalgia for those days, though we had been quite poor during all that time. Valerie and I still regard those as perhaps our happiest days together. There was so much laughter. Sometimes we couldn't sleep for laughing as we went over the madness of what we were trying to create with the group.

We could now afford our first holiday and we rented a house with a swimming pool in Dawlish, Devon, for the occasion. It was May and the weather was not particularly warm, but we did manage to enjoy a swim every day. The boys really loved the freedom of it all and I can still hear little Charlotte giggling away as she was pushed through the water in a big rubber ring. I can also clearly remember Valerie doing a spontaneous dance on the private beach, swaying and twirling, skipping and waving, as if she had suddenly realised that at last she was free to be happy.

We had now settled in to family life and decided that we would get married. We wanted a quiet affair without a party or a reception, as we thought our money could be spent much more wisely. However, we were spotted at the register office as we planned the day. Pierre Moutard, realising what was happening, came over to us. 'You're getting wed, aren't you? You've got to have a party. You've got to do it. It'll be fierce;

it'll be mustard.' So now there was no escaping: we had to have a reception and a party afterwards.

We booked Phil Mahon and his band to play during the evening celebrations and the reception, which was held in the upstairs function room at the Clarence Hotel, in the centre of Bury. Phil had appeared in one of our Interchange Theatre productions and was a well-known blues and soul singer and guitarist around the town. My mum and stepdad, Gerry, had decided to move to Lancashire so that Mum could be nearer to me and my brother, Clive, who was out of the navy and had been living in Barrow-in-Furness and working in the shipyards, but had now moved back to Bury. Also, they were all able to be at the wedding.

The big day finally arrived and Val looked stunning, very beautiful. I again started to feel almost like a normal person. A married man with kids! After the ceremony we had to walk quite a distance through the town in order to get to the Clarence Hotel, and who should be busking in town at the time but Phil Mahon, so he started playing 'Here Comes the Bride', which made quite a spectacle. All of our wedding presents were placed under the table where the food was laid out and the general atmosphere at the reception was one of happiness, with the sun shining, squinting through the big windows. As the evening wore on, Phil's band began playing and little Charlotte got herself right in front and jigged about comically, dancing to the music. She was only 3 years old. Val had done all the catering herself, which was an amazing job, all done on the cheap. It was all going to plan.

The downstairs area of the pub was often frequented by down and outs, old and young, and I didn't want the remainder of the food to go to waste, so I went down and told them that they were welcome to come upstairs if they wanted something to eat. It was only later that we realised they had not only helped themselves to the food, but they had also made off with all our wedding presents. I can only presume that they thought I was rich now that I was appearing more regularly on television. But the truth of the matter was, I still couldn't afford to buy and run a car. Also, Val was still buying some of our clothes from charity shops. Old habits die hard.

Valerie's artistic style was what is generally known as Gallery painting: many abstracts and semi-abstracts, inspired by her inner life and journey. She occasionally got paid to paint a portrait, or someone's dog on a plate, which she didn't really want to do, but she agreed, of course, simply for the money. Despite my acting success at the time, we still could not afford to turn our nose up at any source of income.

John and Nicholas had grown up by now and would soon be leaving school. They wondered what they were going to do for a living and I told them about my time working in kitchens. I said that this was a job where you would never be without something to eat and John decided he would train to be a chef. Some time later he got a job at a Butlin's holiday camp and left home, but when he got there he found that there was little to do in the way of extending his training as a chef, the work mostly consisting of kitchen porter duties. Nicholas played a lot of football and he was shaping into a good striker. He told me of a time when his team had been beaten eleven goals to nil and he remembered that Paul Scholes, who later played for Manchester United, was one of the opposing players.

The Practice was getting around 10 million viewers and by any standards was a successful series. So it came as a massive shock to hear that we wouldn't be making any more episodes. Those with the power and resources had decided to invest the money in a new project, which turned out to be *Albion Market* – a new soap opera, which was popular for a short time during the 1980s. And so square one loomed large in my life once again.

10

Reaching the Bottom

Nothing can bring you peace but yourself.
Ralph Waldo Emerson

What was I going to do now? I had gone from a reasonably good income to nothing. I signed on the dole, again. Valerie had often told me off for over-tipping taxi drivers and bar staff, and now I wished I had all of that money back. During my time in *The Practice* I would chat to other actors about their careers and most of them had done more than me in terms of theatre work, so I decided to ask Libby, my agent, if she could get me some theatre interviews. She did, and I started work at the Oldham Coliseum. The first play I did there was *Harvest in the North*, an obscure and seldom-staged piece. It was to be part of a season of north-country working-class dramas, as we also did *Love on the Dole* and *Spring and Port Wine*.

The artistic director, John Retallack, seemed quite taken with my performances, as he kept asking me to do another play, and then another. I also played Abanazar in the pantomime *Aladdin*. I was gaining much more experience and beginning to feel more and more confident with my all-round range of skills. Oldham Coliseum is a very traditional theatre and had survived the changes to cinemas and bingo halls. They were now about to embark on their centenary production, Shakespeare's *A Midsummer Night's Dream*. John wanted me to play Bottom.

Apart from learning a few speeches at Mountview, I had little knowledge of Shakespeare, and had never performed in a Shakespeare play. There is something about the Bard that demands respect. Many comic actors had played this part and even James Cagney, the great movie actor, had played it in a film version. So I wanted to do justice to this classic role. Bottom is traditionally a loud-mouthed, over-enthusiastic, lovable buffoon and I began wondering if I could give it a different interpretation. In rehearsals I continually experimented with odd ways of performing but eventually John said, 'Steve, Bottom is a big loud-mouth.'

I said, 'I know, but I don't want it all to be on one note.'

'A double bass can play a variety of notes,' said John, and I realised he was right. I had to play a big booming character, but that didn't mean I couldn't be subtle within that.

I had been rehearsing the 'I have had a most rare vision' speech while pacing up and down, but John suggested that I walk to the front of the stage and do the speech there. I told him that I didn't want to look out at the audience, so he suggested that I look above them while delivering the lines, which, though it may have seemed a little contrived at first, did work extremely well. I had difficulties learning the words, even though there aren't a great number, but Shakespeare plays demand plenty of work and I put plenty of effort in. Meriel Scholfield and Malcolm Scates were also in the cast. I had done seven or eight plays with them over the two seasons I had been at the Oldham Coliseum. Jack Ellis was to play Oberon.

When opening night finally arrived, I was very nervous. As I stood in the wings waiting to make my first entrance I said to my ancestors, 'Please be with me and help me through this.' The opening performance proved to be magical, with an equally magical response from the audience. Many who saw it said that the play would easily sell out if it was put on in London and I was very pleased when one kind gentleman told me he had seen eight productions of *A Midsummer Night's Dream* and that mine was the best Bottom he had seen. I wrote to Judi Hayfield, who was one of the casting directors at Granada Television, and asked her to 'come and see my "Bottom" at Oldham'. She accepted the joke and did see the show, bringing along other casting directors. Afterwards, all agreed that ours was a marvellous production.

I was given the chance of performing in another pantomime at Oldham and this time I played King Gorbaduke in *Puss in Boots*.

Because I was now earning much less in theatre work compared to previous television jobs, Val and I began getting behind with the mortgage. One Christmas, spent on the dole, was so bad that we had no money at all for presents. Needing some sort of income other than the dole, I said to Val that I was going to apply for a job as a Santa at the big stores in Manchester. And when your luck is out, it is out. I couldn't even get a job playing Father Christmas. That was a bleak Yuletide for our family.

Our money problems escalated to the point where I didn't have enough to pay the tax man, and we were also getting further and further behind with our mortgage payments. This was hopelessly stressful and soon brought bailiffs to the door. After much sweaty night-time worrying, it seemed that the only way out of our predicament would be to sell the house and pay everybody off in order to avoid bankruptcy, and then to try to take it from there. And that, in the end, is what we did. We had been in the house long enough to get a decent profit on the sale, so the tax was paid and the mortgage arrears were settled, which then left us with approximately ten thousand pounds.

We tried desperately to get a council flat before the sale of our house was finalised, but couldn't and so we were forced to look for something private instead. Luckily we eventually got a house on Spring Street in Bury, from a man who was happy to make an agreement on a handshake, which did away with all of the usual paperwork. 'You pay me forty pounds a week and you can live here as long as you like,' he said, and that was that – what a gentleman. The house was a typical millworker's large terraced house, with two rooms and a kitchen downstairs, and three bedrooms and a bathroom upstairs. We also had a yard at the back of the house and so life moved on in a new direction. A less affluent one, true, but Val and I took it on the chin. The following Christmas was equally bleak and one evening my old mate Alan Roberts knocked on the door and shook my hand, wishing me seasonal greetings. He pressed my hand hard and passed over some money. Knowing my plight, he had come to help me out. It certainly did, at that difficult time. Thanks again, Alphonse. Good mates are rare indeed.

I had done a lot of creative work during my time with the Interchange Theatre Project and so I was now seeing myself perhaps more as a writer than an actor, and I wanted to look the part. After giving this some thought, I went out and bought an old Harris Tweed jacket from a charity shop and also an old pipe. I would stroll around with a book in my pocket as though I was an intellectual. One day I went for a walk alone in my writer's regalia, to my beloved Ashworth Valley, carrying a *Sunday Times* under my arm and puffing away contentedly on the pipe. Making my way through the narrow wooded valley, which was framed by the rock features lining the top of the hills on each side, I sat on a large stone and read the theatre and literary reviews with great interest. I then moved on, easing myself down through the trees towards the path below, but, with a sudden juddering stumble, I lost my footing and started to run uncontrollably. In an effort to remain upright, while clenching the pipe between my teeth and holding on to the *Sunday Times*, I fought desperately with gravity and the rough ground passing rapidly beneath my feet.

I was speeding up and knew all would be lost if I didn't slow myself down somehow, so I tried to grab hold of the branches of a large bush as I rapidly approached, but missed. I was now running down the steep valley side at top speed and couldn't stop myself hurtling into the bushes at the bottom of the hill. Like a free-falling bison I crashed through and came out the other side in a massive flurry of leaves, almost skittling a family who were trying to enjoy a quiet Sunday afternoon stroll. I apologised profusely as one of the children burst into tears and hid behind his mother, but I could not offer an explanation as to why I was running down a steep hill with a pipe clamped between my teeth and frantically waving the *Sunday Times*. To say I was embarrassed is, of course, an understatement, so I slinked away as fast as my trembling, exhausted legs would carry me.

When I got to a little bridge crossing the river that flows through Deepley Vale, I stopped and took a good, long look at myself in the unforgiving depths. It was as if I was seeing myself for the first time. Leaves and twigs were stuck in my hair and that ridiculous pipe was protruding from my mouth. I decided there and then to dispense with the writer image and I violently threw the pipe into the river. Perhaps Ashworth Valley was telling me how pretentious I was becoming again, as it had brought me crashing down to earth, literally and metaphorically, in the past. Perhaps when one is close to nature, it likes to remind us that there is no room for the stupid, pointless ego.

We hired a car and drove around all the run-down areas of Lancashire in search of a cheap house. As we drove slowly through the back streets of Bacup, I heard a loud voice shout,

'F*** off, stranger,' so Val and I decided we would not move to that particular area. However, we did find a run-down house in Burnley. The Burnley Wood Estate was very rough, but the house itself was fine and it suited us, mostly because it only cost £11,000, £1,000 of which we borrowed from my mum. A similar terraced house at that time in Bury would have been in the £20,000 region.

We didn't need to worry too much about the two boys, as Nicholas was working down south and John had his own house. They both had bonny girlfriends and were on the heavy rock scene back in Bury. Our Burnley home was fine for the three of us, but it was basic and needed some repairs carrying out, which we couldn't really afford. Charlotte had soon settled in at the local school and was doing quite well there. In the meantime I managed to get some work at the M6 Theatre Company, based in Rochdale. M6 was, and is, a highly respected group that was, at that time, funded by the Education Authority. The first play I did with them was *Flags and Bandages*, which was set in the Crimean War, primarily covering the life of the amazing Mary Seacole, a black woman who nursed injured soldiers from both sides during that conflict.

We took our plays into schools in and around the borough and provided an educational pack that enabled teachers to do follow-up work on any particular subject which was being covered. We would travel around in a van, build the set, perform the play, dismantle the set, load the van again and then away, either back home or to another school. We would do one show in a morning, and then perform at another school in the afternoon, or sometimes we did two performances at the same school. Eileen Murphy was the artistic director and Dorothy Wood was co-ordinator. There was a permanent cast of five actors. Jim Byrne and Maggie Tagney were two of the regulars. The company would also put on a Christmas show, which was performed in a very traditional family panto style, but without any sexual innuendos or cheap gags. We would always tell a story that had a moral tale threaded through it. I got the chance to play Abanazar again, but this was a much darker version, more suited to *Arabian Nights*. Neil Duffield, who is Eileen Murphy's husband, often wrote the pieces we performed. While I was busy with the theatre work, Valerie made some new friends in Burnley and became involved in art projects in the town. She also took up an interest in the Labour movement.

We were back to being quite poor, but we were happy enough and Charlotte, to our great relief, seemed to be thriving at school, having her own little group of friends. We lived a few doors from Tony Abbott, one of the many brothers of Paul Abbott, the creator of the popular television series *Shameless*. Although we were okay generally, in some ways life in our new town was very worrying, as the estate was home to a number of heroin addicts and we were obviously concerned about the kind of influences Charlotte would grow up surrounded by. Val wasn't too keen on going out in the evening, but I began frequenting the Woodman pub, which was just around the corner from where we lived. I got to know a few of the locals and was soon nicknamed Out of Work Actor, as I would often be asking if anyone could lend me a tenner till the weekend.

I did some more work for the M6 Theatre, but between jobs I signed on. One day I had gone to re-register on the dole when a very disturbed man began arguing with one of the staff, protesting that he wasn't sick and that he wanted to work. I turned to see who was making all this fuss and the chap caught sight of me. He then ran over and grabbed my hair, pulling me around the room. I tried to stay calm, but warned him that I would knock him out if he didn't let go. He wouldn't let go, but just as I was about to drop him, one of the staff jumped in and got him round the neck, pulling him to the ground. The police were called and they asked if I wished to make a formal complaint, but I said no, as the poor chap was obviously disturbed. I then said, 'Burnley seems to use very extreme ways of getting people *not* to sign on the dole,' and almost everyone laughed, breaking the tension.

A teenage boy lived next door and his bedroom was right next to Charlotte's little room. He was constantly on CB radio late at night and the noise often prevented young Charlotte from sleeping, so I had been round on several occasions and complained to his mother. I asked politely that the noise be stopped, but they just ignored me. I decided I would try just one more time and then, if the noise didn't stop, I would resort to more extreme measures. His mother just excused him, more or less saying that 'boys will be boys', but I politely asked her to tell him not to go on too late. Again, they took no notice.

One night, at half past midnight, Charlotte was again being prevented from getting her sleep, so I grabbed an old golf club I had in the living room and went and reached out from our front door and smashed their front window with it, before easing myself back inside. I was then forced to do some unpaid acting, as the mother came round.

'What happened?' I asked, feigning ignorance and surprise.

'Someone has smashed our front window,' said the mother.

I told her that it was probably someone who couldn't get any peace because of the CB radio being on all night, saying that other people, as well as myself, had been complaining about the noise. The police were called and they knocked on our door. I just said that someone must have smashed it because of the disturbance at night.

'It wasn't you then?' asked the officer.

'No, not me, but someone,' I said. The matter was left there and my more extreme measures worked, as we weren't disturbed any more.

We were doing a play for the M6 Theatre called *Operation Elvis* and this production gave me the chance to play drums again. The story was about a day out for a boy who was suffering from cerebral palsy; it was punctuated by music and, as you would expect, given the title, several Elvis numbers featured. I played the part of Jacky, who was a country character with a broad northern accent. I also played panto at times and this meant that Christmas was a magical time for Charlotte, as she was delighted to see Dad appearing on stage. She got the chance to go backstage, as well as actually on stage for the sing-along parts of the show. And so the world of theatre became very familiar to her, though she would get upset whenever I played the baddie, simply because when I came to take the curtain call I would be universally booed and hissed. She was fine about it once I explained that this was all part of the pantomime fun.

Whilst sitting in the library in Burnley one wet, miserable dole day, I read in a newspaper that the Royal Exchange Theatre in Manchester were holding a playwriting competition and that the winner would receive a cash prize, together with their play being staged at the theatre. Perhaps I can keep the hyenas at bay by winning that, I thought to myself. So I set about trying to write a tale about the depression and unemployment the north-west was suffering at the time. I had been thinking for years of writing a play centred on bottle digging, finding period bottles and artefacts that have monetary value, as Bury was then the bottle digging capital of the world. This play, I thought, would give me a chance to combine this feature of north-west life with the unemployment and poverty that was part of everyday life for many in the area.

Having worked in industry many times myself, I was deeply concerned about the rapid decline of the region's manufacturing base. Like so many local people, I had experienced first-hand the problems wrought by unemployment, debt and repossession. What was of more concern to me was that nobody seemed to be making too much of an effort to tackle and solve such problems. There just seemed to be a general attitude of,

'Well, that's the way it is,' and nobody was saying, 'But does it have to be this way?' This apathy seemed to be rife in the world of theatre and television too, as no one had really portrayed the effect of this on human lives since Alan Bleasdale's amazing *Boys from the Blackstuff*.

The play I was putting together was about an unemployed 50-year-old who was turning more and more to drink in an effort to cope with being out of work, with little, if any, prospects for the future. His wife, as well as running the home, was trying to improve her lot by getting a degree as a mature student. These characters were obviously based on Valerie and myself and Val helped a lot during my research and writing of the piece, in spite of her busy life. Valerie had been doing some work as a cleaner, as trying to manage on the dole is, as many will know, not easy.

Before sending my play to the Royal Exchange Theatre, I asked Eileen Murphy at the M6 Theatre Company to read it and tell me honestly what she thought. She liked it and I was asked if the M6 could perform the play for their community tour of the North-West. I was thrilled. They were prepared to pay me a commissioning fee in order to stage it, but this presented a problem, as part of the criteria for the competition was that it had not to have been performed professionally – I could not send it in to the Royal Exchange if M6 produced it. However, at least I would be guaranteed to make some money from it and so I agreed to the M6 putting on the play.

Whilst writing this epic, I would go to the library in the town centre almost every day to hand-write the script, as I couldn't use a typewriter. I had to research the history of pot production in order to get my facts right. I wrote the end of the play first, then the beginning, with the in-between sections being the most difficult to conjure in my imagination. I read sections to Valerie and she would make constructive comments and suggestions. Sometimes I would get up during the middle of the night in order to write down ideas before I forgot them. This went on for weeks and its creation possessed me the whole time. It became an obsession and, when working at home, I would constantly stop writing, roll a cigarette, light it and inhale deeply, attempting to calm what almost felt like creative madness. I couldn't smoke in the library, so I got on better when I worked there and was finally able to finish the play. I can remember writing down those last few words and then walking out into the sunshine with tears in my eyes, muttering to myself, 'I've done it, I've done it.'

I had written a three-hour play and felt that I could now call myself a true playwright. I felt that I had paid my dues to the theatre tradition, though the experience had been incredibly painful, as well as joyful; painful because I had used many of our own bad experiences as a basis for the play. *All My Joy*, I'm happy to say, was generally a critical success and the money we got for it helped us out of a hole.

Some of the work I did with the M6 Theatre Company in Rochdale was less serious stuff, such as when we put on *The Ugly Duckling*, a new Christmas show. One day we had performed two shows and on my way home I called in at a pub at Todmorden, which was where I changed buses on my journey between Rochdale and Burnley. I meant to stay and have just a few pints and then catch a later bus home, but, in an ale-induced reverie, I lost track of time, which meant that I missed the last bus. I tried to persuade a taxi driver to take me home, but he wanted the money upfront and I didn't have enough on me. I said that I would go in the house and get him the money when we reached home, but he refused. I was very, very drunk at the time. He obviously suspected that I would do a runner once I got back to Burnley.

I telephoned Val from a phone box and told her of my predicament, and I assured her that I would somehow find a way home. I would try another taxi firm. Then I kept ringing her to let her know how I was getting on and she got so mad with me for disturbing her sleep that she hung up and went back to bed. Having failed to get a lift home, I decided I would walk back to the M6 Theatre base in Rochdale, ready for the morning show. Rochdale was nearer than Burnley, so it made sense to walk there – a journey of about 9 miles. The morning show was scheduled for nine-thirty and I was certain I could make it. The rain began pouring down as I trudged along the dark, empty road, the bleak swell of the Pennine moors looming all around me. After several miles, I noticed lights were on in a factory and realised that the night shift would now be well under way. So I crept in through a side door and lay on some bales, resting and attempting to dry off. I had been soaked, literally, to the skin.

After an hour or so I knew I had to carry on my journey and reluctantly headed off once more into the unceasing rain. The darkness and the crowding swell of hills only served to darken my mood as I mulled over this life in my manic-depressive state, all the time feeling sorry for Val because she had me to put up with. I finally arrived at the M6 base at around 6 a.m. and used my key to get in. I managed to dry off to some extent, and then I got a bus to Middleton, where I was to give my Mr Fox morning performance. I discovered that Gordon Wiseman, a short, rotund actor who played Mr Rooster, had also had a heavy session on the drink during the previous evening. So his performance, like mine, was not of the best. During the interval I saw him in the wings as he exclaimed, 'Tragedy, tragedy! Nose fell off!' He forlornly stared at his hand, which had in it a squashed piece of putty. Not only that, but he also mistakenly referred to Doris Duck as Doris Dick in front of a couple of hundred school kids. Doris Duck, incidentally, was played by Jane Cox.

For my part I sweated more than usual in my fur fox costume and, because it couldn't be washed and dried in time for the next performance, I became known to all and sundry as Stinker until the end of the run.

11

End in Sight

The answer is in the motion of a falling leaf, to be seen but never retained, to be understood, but never explained.
Steve Halliwell

Empty days returned as things again slumped in Burnley, which meant that Val and I seemed to be drifting further and further apart. Neither of us had regular work and my vision of a successful acting career was rapidly fading yet again. My agent, Libby Glenn, had sadly died of cancer some years earlier and I was now with Manchester's leading agent, Barbara Pemberton. But things were rather barren on the work front, which was obviously affecting our personal life. I resorted more and more to Kestrel Super Strength lager as the cheapest ticket to oblivion, and Val, unbeknownst to me, was on Prozac because of her depression. The physical side of our relationship was by now non-existent and I was drunk more and more frequently as the weeks and months passed. It is a strange thing, but heavy drinkers often feel that it is only they who are suffering, and not the people they live with. I was no exception and I failed to realise what pressure I was putting on Val and young Charlotte.

Valerie was also missing her sons. She told me she needed to visit them more often, but as we had no car it was a two-bus journey to see them. I rarely went along when Val visited. Having been without a father myself from an early age, I didn't really know what my role should be with regard to Valerie's sons now that they had grown up and left home. I know now the obvious answer was just to care about them and be there for them, but back then I always had a way of putting my needs ahead of theirs. Added emotional pressure was then put on Valerie as her dad, Jim, sadly, but not unexpectedly, died of prostate cancer. It was a devastating blow for her. Her dad had given Val her only sense of security, as her mum had suffered with multiple sclerosis and consequently spent long periods in hospital. She had eventually died when Valerie was just 17.

All of this meant that Valerie became deeply depressed and I was too depressed myself to be of any use to her. She needed a rock and I failed her. This was a vicious cycle, because I needed someone to lean on, and Val was in too bad a state to be that rock for me. And so, in the end, we both stopped fighting to save our relationship. It is easy to say, with hindsight, that we should have stuck it out and pulled through those bad times together, but we had both been drained of energy and had nothing left for the struggle. Life seemed to be endlessly hostile and the pair of us were consumed by feelings of hopelessness.

The depression I suffered lost its mania and seemed permanent. The effect of Prozac on Val meant that she had lost some of her sensitive and compassionate qualities, which I badly needed at the time. Things became so bad that, in the end, Val said that she was moving out and going back to Bury. Our daughter, Charlotte, must have been feeling the strain too, because she didn't object at all when her mother told her they were moving out. Charlotte had missed her brothers and we reassured her that she would still see her dad at weekends. We talked such important matters through and parted without any big argument. I tried to be philosophical about the whole thing, but my sense of failure was immense. A second marriage had failed in my pursuit of that elusive career success.

This led me to think that maybe actors should not try to build real relationships, because part of their emotional life remains on hold for when it is needed in a role. Maybe emotional commitment, in the fullest sense, isn't possible if an actor is to do their job properly. Emotion has to be stored away deep inside in readiness for that big scene they will one day perform. These were just a few of the things I mulled over during those dark and difficult days, when the future, even life itself, beyond the bottom of a glass of ale that is, held little appeal for me. I didn't know where to turn for help and in the end I said a deep prayer to God, The Oneness, The Singularity, The Tao, however we choose to describe it. I asked for help so that I could make some money and at least then be able to help support others, as I seemed incapable of offering emotional support to my family at that particular time in my life.

After Val and Charlotte had left our home in Burnley, I sank to an even lower level of depression, trying not to show it to Charlotte, however, when I met her at weekends. I would take her into Burnley town centre, where I routinely treated her to chocolate fudge cake, which she loved. She also enjoyed going to Turf Moor, where we cheered the Claret and Blues, Burnley Football Club. At half-time we would always have meat and potato pies and cups of tea. I was heartbroken every time I put her on the bus home, where she was met at the other end by Valerie. My whole life seemed a complete mess and I began wondering more and more if I was deluding myself about ever having a successful acting career. Kestrel Super Strength was still my medication and by way of escape I spent too much time with Mick Heywood and the rest of the lads in the Woodman pub. Our pub quiz team was called The Entertainers, and included Barry Yates, an old mate from Bury who was living in Burnley. Also, a guy we called Stevie Ears, who had, of course, the sticking-out cab door lugs.

When out of work and signing on, I often had time to kill during the day and I would sometimes play pitch and putt in Townley Park with Stevie Ears. Stevie had been a coach driver, but had been forced to retire for a time due to health problems. He had only one kidney. Stopping at the fourteenth hole one morning, he told me that he had once died – for a short time, that is, before eventually being revived by the doctors. He described to me his out-of-body experience: the white light, the peace he had felt, how a voice had given him the choice of whether to live or die. He chose to live, he told me, because he was worried about leaving his wife and the dog. But he also admitted that he was tempted to give up and go towards the light instead.

After a few more months on the dole, and a few poorly paid training videos, I eventually auditioned for a part in a play being produced by the Hull Truck Theatre Company. They offered me a six-month tour of Britain, but because of my marriage break-up and the situation with seeing Charlotte at weekends I felt I couldn't take it. In the end I asked my agent to just put me forward for TV work; she was a bit put out at this, as I had just turned down six months' wages, of which she would have got a percentage. However, I stood my ground, as the break-up had affected Charlotte and if I had gone away for six months, who knows how this would have affected her.

A few more months passed and only small jobs came my way, which were, again, mostly poorly paid training videos. But then, out of the blue, I got a phone call from my agent telling me that Sue Jackson, the casting director for Yorkshire Television, wanted me to go for an interview/audition for a new character in Emmerdale. Sue had seen me many times on stage so she knew what I could do. This character was to be called Zak Dingle and he was a petty criminal and a pig farmer who had been a bare-knuckle fighter in his younger days. He was scripted to have a fight with Ned Glover, who was a regular character in the show. The job was for just two episodes. I certainly wanted to be seen for the part, as the character sounded great – not unlike some of the people I had known back in Bury.

I travelled over the Pennines to Yorkshire; Stevie Ears kindly drove me and Charlotte, who was staying with me at the time. I auditioned, along with six other actors, some of whom I had come to know quite well, as we were often being seen for the same parts. Although my nose had been broken during my earlier days, I didn't look as much of a bare-knuckle fighter as some of the other guys, so I was up against it. Having arrived in Leeds early, Stevie, Charlotte and I sat in the studio canteen and I went over and over my audition scene with them, trying to get it as perfect as possible.

My own character is quite different to that of Zak, as I am quite softly spoken and do not naturally come over as a tough, ex-boxer type. So I could not just be myself in the interview. In fact, I based the character on a bloke I had known in the past, though his identity shall remain a secret. I asked to stand up for the reading, and did quite a bit of pointing and threatening, which I aimed at Mervyn Watson, the producer. They then asked if I had any objection to rolling into a river during the fight scene in the second episode and I said that I had none, that, in fact, I would love it. A chance to play a real cowboy-like scene would be a dream come true for me. When it was all over, I felt that I had given it my best shot. I badly wanted this part, but all I could do now was to return home to Burnley, where I would spend an agonising time waiting to hear if I had got the job or not. Sometimes this period of stress can run into days, even weeks. Part of me was positive, sensing that this was maybe my destiny being played out. But then negative thoughts would take over as I remembered that I had been mistaken in the past about such things.

The next few days were very long and painful, but eventually the phone call came from Barbara. I listened as my agent delivered the news, and then, I cried, 'Yes! Yes! Yes! I got the job! I got the job!' True, it was only two episodes, but I now had a chance, a chance to make my mark. My life, I felt, had been plagued with failures, but this time it was going to be different. It had to be!

In the second of my two episodes, there was to be a bareknuckle fight and the stunt co-ordinator was putting us through our paces in order to make sure we didn't hurt each other. Johnny Leese, an ex-comedian and singer who had broken into acting a long time before I met him, played Ned Glover, who my character was to fight. The fight scene was to end with us both rolling into the river and Zak Dingle would eventually be beaten. During the actual fight scene my character had to kick his opponent in the groin and Johnny wore a metal plate strapped to the inside of his leg for protection, which I was to aim for. I had to be precise, because if I'd got my aim wrong he would have received a swift and very painful kick in the balls and forever after would have sung like a choirboy.

Apart from the scene in the river, the fight sequences had to be repeated several times over so that they could be covered from various angles. This meant that Johnny was kicked hard on at least six occasions. We wore wet suits under our clothing and when we eventually took them off Johnny turned to me and said, 'Steve, look.' There was a purple bruise on the inside of his leg, the size of a saucer. The poor man hadn't said a word during filming, but those kicks must have really hurt.

'Oh Johnny, I am so sorry, mate,' I said.

But he just shrugged his shoulders and said, 'I suffered a lot more pain than this doing stand-up comedy.' What a star!

Johnny had made me feel very welcome from the minute I arrived until the minute I had finished those two episodes, and I will always be grateful to him for that.

I felt that I tried my best, and that there was really nothing more that I could have done to make my chances of getting future work any better. Not only had I acted my heart out, but I had also got on well with the cast, crew and the director, so I was sad to be leaving. I hoped I had made enough of an impression to get more work on *Emmerdale*, but about a week had passed and still the phone hadn't rung. Then a few days later my agent called and told me that they would be offering me a few more episodes, which welcome news filled me with a deep inner joy. Barbara also told me that I would be screen-testing with several actresses in order to find Zak a wife.

Butch Dingle (Paul Loughran) was already in the programme, but Sam and Tina, Zak's other two children, were still to be cast. Sandra Gough, who had become famous playing Irma Ogden in *Coronation Street*, was given the role of Nelly, Zak's wife. During my screen-test with her she had walked into the room, gone straight up to Mervyn Watson and said, 'What star sign are you? I'm not sure I can work with you.' She was very much her own woman and very eccentric.

Sam and Tina were to be played by two young gifted actors, James Hooton and Jackie Pirie. And so the Dingle family was born. Later, I was taken to see the Dingle homestead, Wishing Well Cottage. This, I felt, definitely had to be my destiny, what I had been heading towards for all those years. My knowledge and experience of backstreet life, the fights, the poverty, the daily struggles I was so familiar with, all stood me in good stead for this character. I knew well the world of the Dingle family. I was thrilled by this great career break, yet still carried an inner sadness in my heart, as my real-life family had disintegrated around me. Still, this was an answered prayer, as I was going to be able to help ease the pain financially. Yorkshire

Television had given me the break I'd dreamed of since I first picked up *The Stage* newspaper all those years ago and I will be eternally grateful to them for that. Also, I owe many drinks to Jeff Naylor, the director who first cast me as Zak Dingle.

Postscript

The only really valuable thing is intuition.

Albert Einstein

It was great to have more acting work to look forward to and especially to be playing this character, yet, in spite of all that, something was missing. I still didn't feel quite right about the way Zak Dingle looked. I was chatting to Stan Richards about this and he told me that when he found his woolly hat to complement his big mutton-chop sideburns, he knew that he had got the look for his character, the legendary Seth Armstrong. 'Get thee-sen a cap, lad. Get thee-sen a cap,' were his words of wisdom. And so I set out in search of the right look for Zak.

After many failed attempts at finding the right headgear, I wandered into a charity shop in Burnley town centre and there, hanging up on a peg, was an old flat cap that I felt might just do the trick. I bent and battered it about a bit, in an attempt to give it the look I wanted. A man's cap was a very personal thing when I was growing up and the owners grew very fond of them, Fred Dibnah being a perfect example.

At the television studio back in Leeds, I looked into the mirror of the dressing room and placed the black corduroy cap on my head – it hit me. At last I knew what I would be doing for the next few years. I hadn't yet been offered any kind of long-term contract, but I knew that I was armed with enough acting experience and enough life experience to make this character my signature role.

Looking into the mirror then was so very different to when I had looked into that mirror at the Wash and Brush-Up in Trafalgar Square, all those years ago. I knew who I was and where my destiny lay. My life had been packed full of ups and downs, but now it all seemed to make sense. Everything I had been through had equipped me for this character, who, I was determined, would represent the under classes in a truthful way. Many people would like to have a meaningful place in society, but circumstances of birth make that almost impossible for them. I hoped I could help give them a voice. I do hope that my struggles and eventual success will inspire and encourage people to keep reaching out for their dreams. Zak was a backstreet boxer and small-time scrap dealer and he used these skills to try to survive and feed his family.

Boxing has always been a way out from oppression and poverty. The Jews, the Italians, the Irish and, of course, the descendants of African slaves, have made some of the greatest boxers we have ever seen. The scrap metal industry has been a good way out of poverty for many who live in industrial countries.

Zak Dingle would be an example of a family man who continually struggles to climb up from the bottom rungs of society's ladder. He would be a man with a good heart and an unceasing tryer. Yes, the cap did fit, and yes, I am still wearing it.

I know there are no errors,
In the great Eternal plan,
And all things work together,
For the final good of man,
And I know when my soul speeds onward,
In its grand Eternal quest,
I shall say as I look back earthward,
Whatever is – is best.

From a poem by Ella W. Wilcox

Appendix 1

Quotes from Published Reviews

'I am proud that my critical career should conclude with so fine a play as George Thatcher's *The Only Way Out* ... Not since William Douglas Home's epoch-making *Now Barabbas* has there been a play about a condemned man that is so profoundly moving and so exquisitely acted as *The Only Way Out*.'

Harold Hobson, *Sunday Times*, 1976 on *The Only Way Out*

'The most convincing performance came from Steve Halliwell as Hindley. His portrayal of the drunken brute, culminating in a dramatic death scene, was the most outstanding for a long time.'

John Wallace, *Guardian*, 1987 on *Wuthering Heights*

'Steve Halliwell gives the boorish "Bottom" his best Oldham accent and, with a fine array of facial contortions, steals every scene he's in.'

Guy Nelson, *Independent*, 1987 on *A Midsummer Night's Dream*

'Inspired by anger at the "senseless waste of the world's most valuable asset, people", the play is potent material for this M6 Theatre Company tour of the region Steve Halliwell is writing about because it urges not only understanding but positive action against inertia and despair.'

Francesca Turner, *Guardian*, 1980s on *All My Joy* tour

'Steve Halliwell, giving one of his best performances as the cynical world weary teacher.'

Natalie Anglesey, *Stage*, 1987 on *No More Sitting on the Old School Bench*

Appendix 2

All My Joy

An extract from the play *All My Joy* by Steve Halliwell.

JIMMY: They're not corny … read it Moreen.
         Read it out loud!!

MOREEN: 'This trifle it from me you take
           And keep it for the giver's sake.
           You'll see when ere you look
                                    within
           What all my joy is centred in.'

               SHE TURNS IT OVER

JIMMY: Polished   metal.   Do   you   see
         yourself?

                 PAUSE

MOREEN: I look tired.

JIMMY: Go and have a lie down for a while.

MOREEN: I haven't time!! Have you got a
          buyer for it?

JIMMY: The lid? Oh? No problem!!
          Geoffrey's dealer's been calling
          round regular, seeing when I'll
          sell. He's being a bit cagey about
          how much it's worth. I just wanted
          to hang on 'til you'd seen it. I
          thought you might want to keep it?
          And I'd pay Joey off.

MOREEN: It's a nice little thing … but if
          you can sell it then that's what
          you'll have to do. If you could
          get enough just to have the phone
          put back on. I did want to get
          away but I also wanted to be able
          to contact you! Why is everything
          always so hard!! It all seemed so
          easy for those young students.
          They have money problems of course
          … but most of them seem to breeze
          along … Money worries all the
          time! Worries about you and David
          … still, almost over. My thesis
          is in. Just two more paintings to
          finish and then the degree show,
          and that's it!

                    PAUSE

                    184

JIMMY: It was alright in the old days, you didn't have all that work and worry then, when I was in engineering.

MOREEN: LAUGHS. Oh Jimmy!! … I still had David right from the start. I should have been doing all this then. Working towards a Fine Art Degree, instead of changing nappies!

JIMMY: You loved being pregnant! You used to walk round proud as punch as if you were the only girl in the world who'd ever had a baby … I used to help with the nappies anyway!! Not many blokes did that in them days.

MOREEN: I was happy in a way. I did what I had to do.

JIMMY: Is that all it was? Duty?

PAUSE

MOREEN: Alright! I was young and in love!! Is that what you want to hear? … I was … young and in love … but there was always a sense of loss as well … always top in art at school I was!

JIMMY: Ay! You've told me a thousand times … that's what you say to me! PAUSE.

Well at least you're doing it now.
Something you always wanted to do.
You've had another chance … wish I
could get one.

MOREEN: You could do something, you're
not stupid, really, except when
you're on that! Which seems to
be permanently now … look at you
… you're like a baby with his
bottle. You all think you're such
characters, don't you? I've seen
plenty of you when I worked behind
bars … such characters!! The only
trouble is you're all the same
bloody one! Big fighting, drinking,
hard men. It's a joke! What are you
so afraid of? You act like you're
ready for anything and you're
ready for nothing!

JIMMY: Shut up!! What do you know!

MOREEN: What is it you're so afraid of?
… Those young lads at University
don't have to play tough guy. They
can be sensitive and caring. They
can …

JIMMY: They're all middle class that's
why!! Cossetted!!

MOREEN: There you go again.

JIMMY: What? What? … What is it now?

MOREEN: Even the working class boys are
          not afraid to say they don't like
          violence. They don't need to act
          tough. They treat all that as a
          joke. Just a joke!!

JIMMY: They haven't had to do it, have
          they?

MOREEN: Do what?

JIMMY: Work! Or if they have done any
          they've escaped it!!

MOREEN: Escaped what?

JIMMY: SHOUTS. Being hard!! Working hard!!
          Hard graft amongst hard men. You
          have to be hard or you're no use.
          If you're not strong and you can't
          stick it, long hard boring work,
          then you're no use!! You can't be
          soft in that world! … You'd have
          had no bloody university buildings
          without men like that!!

MOREEN: But why not just do something
          else? Something more creative!
          Fulfilling?

JIMMY: Moreen? … That's not you talking
          is it? That's those people you're

listening to over there. You know
how it was in towns like this when
we were growing up. If you didn't
pass your eleven plus you were
factory fodder.

ALL MY JOY

M6 THEATRE COMPANY ROCHDALE

by Steve Halliwell

JIMMY SMITH	Carl Davies
MAUREEN SMITH	Maggie Tagney
DAVID SMITH	James Byrne
	Paul Oldham
JOEY	Keith Ladd
GEOFFREY	
	EILEEN MURPHY
Director	DEE SIDWELL
Designer	RUTH SIDERY
Sound & Light	COLIN CUTHBERT

"*All My Joy* is in some way a poem dedicated to my family and friends, and especially to the memory of Jim Murphy.

Since childhood I have hated to see the endless sight of unfulfilled human potential. To my mind the biggest ecological crime of all is the senseless waste of the world's most valuable asset, people."

— Steve Halliwell

ALL MY JOY ON STAGE

Spring Community Tour Dates 1993

February 23 - April 3

ALL MY JOY ON TOUR

FEBRUARY

Tues 23	7.30	ROCHDALE, *Hamer C.P. School*	0706 - 355898
Weds 24	8.00	BURY, *The Met Arts Centre*	061 - 761 - 2216
Thurs 25	7.30	STALYBRIDGE, *Copley Community Centre*	061 - 338 - 6230
Fri 26	7.30	ST. HELENS, *Citadel Arts Centre*	0744 - 35436

MARCH

Mon 1	7.30	CHESTER, *Chester College*	0244 - 375444
Tues 2	7.30	LITTLEBOROUGH, *L'bro Community School*	0706 - 377475
Weds 3	7.30	BOLTON, *Octagon Studio Theatre*	0204 - 20661
Thurs 4	2.00/7.30	BOLTON, *Octagon Studio Theatre*	0204 - 20661
Fri 5	7.30	BOLTON, *Octagon Studio Theatre*	0204 - 20661
Sat 6	7.30	BOLTON, *Octagon Studio Theatre*	0204 - 20661
Mon 8	1.45	STRETFORD, *Stretford High School*	061 - 876 - 4734
Tues 9	7.30	CREWE, *South Cheshire College*	0270 - 69133, x287
Weds 10	4.30	MANCHESTER, *Arden Centre, South Manchester Community College*	061 - 957 - 1716
		at	061 - 957 - 1730
Thurs 11	4.15/7.30	OLDHAM, *Sixth Form College*	061 - 628 - 8000
Fri 12	7.30	CASTLETON, *Castleton Community Centre*	0706 - 49351
Tues 16	1.45/7.30	ROCHDALE, *Gracie Fields Theatre*	0706 - 353643
Weds 17	7.30	STOCKPORT, *The Ridge College*	061 - 427 - 7733
Thurs 18	7.30	RUNCORN, *Shopping City Library Theatre*	0928 - 715351
Fri 19	7.30	SALFORD, *Hulton High School*	061 - 790 - 4214
Sat 20	7.30	ORMSKIRK, *Cross Hall Arts Theatre*	0695 - 572625
Mon 22	7.30	WAKEFIELD, *Bretton Hall College*	0924 - 830261
Tues 23	8.00	LIVERPOOL, *Unity Theatre*	051 - 709 - 4988
Thurs 25	2.15/7.30	HEYWOOD, *Hopwood Civic Hall*	0706 - 368130
Tues 30	1.30/7.30	BURNLEY, *Towneley High School*	0282 - 30055
Weds 31	7.30	LEIGH, *Leigh Drama Centre*	0942 - 605258

APRIL

Thurs 1	3.45	ALSAGER, *Alsager Comprehensive School*	0270 - 873221
Fri 2	2.00/7.30	MIDDLETON, *Middleton Civic Hall*	061x 643 - 2389
Sat 3	7.30	HUDDERSFIELD, *Marsden Mechanics*	0484 - 430808

Details of all performances available from M6 Theatre, Hamer C.P. School, Albert Royds Street, Rochdale OL16 2SU, or (0706) 355898

"I wanted to write something which would show life as it is in the north west but also inspire people"

STEVE HALLIWELL AND ALL MY JOY

It is in the summer that M6, like most theatre companies, decides its programme for the year ahead. For the spring community tour this involves the company members researching a selection of plays and deciding how they would be received by the sizeable community audience that M6 has built up over the years. Usually one play leaps out during the research and the decision makes itself; this is how the two previous community tours of Blood Brothers and Operation Elvis came to be.

Last summer, however, there had been no such flashes of collective inspiration. Having scheduled two brand-new pieces of writing for the autumn, the company had been looking for an extant play to take on the spring tour. During this period of impasse one of their number produced a script which Steve Halliwell, a local actor who had worked with M6 for years, had given her for a friendly opinion. Steve was intending entering the script, a passionate and very long piece called This Trifle, for the prestigious Mobil playwriting competition. But after the company had read it through the inspiration had arrived; this had to be the next M6 community tour.

"I had been thinking for years about the possibility of writing a play around bottle-digging," says Steve Halliwell, who is based in Burnley but is a native of Bury, renowned amongst those who know as the bottle-digging capital of the north-west. "But it was only in about March 1992 that I started connecting it to an issue-based play such as this has become."

Steve had been increasingly concerned at the decline of his beloved north-west. Having worked in industry himself, the decline of the region's manufacturing base was a concern to him, and his family, like so many locally, had experienced at first hand some of the problems of unemployment, debt and repossession which are covered in All My Joy. "What really concerned me was that nobody seemed to be fighting these problems. There was a general attitude of 'that's the way it is', and nobody was saying, 'but does it have to be?'

"This apathy seemed to be there in the arts as well. Television and the theatre have not done much on the effect of these problems on human lives since Boys From the Blackstuff," he adds. "In All My Joy there are allegorical things which people can pick up on if they want, but it is very much about people not fighting back enough. As it turned out, as soon as the play was finished people

started demonstrating about the fate of the miners, so perhaps it was not quite as needed as I thought!

All My Joy is a play made rich by the interweaving of many different strands of strong themes and strong characters; there is a lot more going on than in most new writing, and this is entirely interthogal, despite making a "mammoth task" for writing, reading, and working on.

"I just felt that it would be a richer, more three-dimensional affair," explains Steve Halliwell. "I wanted to write about people with plenty about them and their lives;

Members of the ALL MY JOY cast in rehearsal with Steve Halliwell and Eileen Murphy

with more of an identity than the sketchy stereotypes it would have been easy to create when dealing with issues like these. People don't relate to facts and statistics; they relate to other people. It is the little idiosyncracies and dreams of these characters that makes you feel the tragedy of their lives more deeply."

One fact which may appear in the play concerns the possible discovery and theft of a method of pot lid transfer printing in

the eighteenth-century West Midlands. The idea of an unknown enameller who had worked before the official discovery of this method is based on some truth. The fact that Christie's would neither confirm nor deny this possibility adds to the dramatic effect of an allegorical situation which, if not true, is certainly possible.

Although Steve Halliwell has been an actor for years, and has worked on his own plays before with theatre workshops and unemployed centres, this is his first play which has been produced professionally. He found the process of editing "not nearly as daunting as I thought it would be. Authorship of a play is a collaborative effort, and by working with Eileen and the cast the lines and momentum of the play work better than before."

Tackling issues such as unemployment, debt, alcoholism, repossession and despair could easily have led to a strong but thoroughly depressing piece. All My Joy, however, is laced with humour and hope. "I didn't want to be negative about the lives of these strong and adaptable individuals," says Steve. "I wanted to write something which would show life as it is in the north west but also inspire people.

"I want to say, 'let's remember who we are and what we and our ancestors have done. Yes, there are problems around and life can be hard to us, but we are strong, vibrant people, and let's fight it.'"

THE MAKING OF ALL MY JOY

THE MAKING OF ALL MY JOY